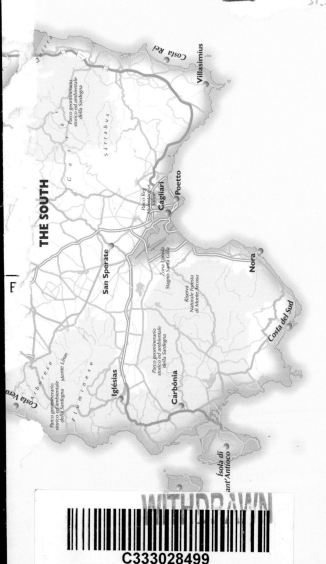

THE SOUTH

Costa Rei

Villasimius

Cágliari

Poetto

Parco geominerario
storico ed ambientale
della Sardegna

Sárrabus

Parco Reg
Molentargius
Saline

San Sperate

Zona Umida
Stagno Santa Gilla

Riserva
Naturale Foresta
di Monte Arcosu

Nora

Costa del Sud

Parco geominerario
storico ed ambientale
della Sardegna

Iglésias

Monte Linas

Carbónia

Costa Verde

Parco geominerario
storico ed ambientale
della Sardegna

Isola di
ant'Antíoco

TWINPACK
Sardinia

BARBARA RADCLIFFE ROGERS AND STILLMAN ROGERS

AA Publishing

If you have any comments or suggestions for this guide you can contact the editor at
travelguides@TheAA.com

How to Use This Book

KEY TO SYMBOLS

✚ Map reference

✉ Address

☎ Telephone number

🕐 Opening/closing times

🍴 Restaurant or café

🚆 Nearest railway station

🚌 Nearest bus route

⛴ Nearest ferry route

♿ Facilities for visitors with disabilities

❓ Other practical information

▷ Further information

ℹ Tourist information

✋ Admission charges:
Expensive (over €9),
Moderate (€6–€9), and
Inexpensive (under €6)

★ Major Sight   ★ Minor Sight

👣 Walks   🚍 Drives

🎁 Shops

🎭 Entertainment and Activities

🍴 Restaurants

This guide is divided into four sections

• Essential Sardinia: An introduction to the island and tips on making the most of your stay.
• Sardinia by Area: We've broken the island into five areas, and recommended the best sights, shops, activities, restaurants, entertainment and nightlife venues in each one. Suggested walks and drives help you to explore.
• Where to Stay: The best hotels, whether you're looking for luxury, budget or something in between.
• Need to Know: The info you need to make your trip run smoothly, including getting about by public transport, weather tips, emergency phone numbers and useful websites.

Navigation In the Sardinia by Area chapter, we've given each area its own colour, which is also used on the locator maps throughout the book and the map on the inside front cover.

Maps The fold-out map accompanying this book is a comprehensive map of Sardinia. The grid on this fold-out map is the same as the grid on the locator maps within the book. The grid references to these maps are shown with capital letters, for example A1. The grid references to the town plans are shown with lower-case letters, for example a1.

Contents

CONTENTS

Introducing Sardinia

Sardinia is a land of many contrasts: long white sand beaches and huge mountains; ancient stone towers and Renzo Piano architecture; the newness of smart resorts and folk festivals whose ancient origins are lost in time.

Most visitors come for Sardinia's incomparable beaches, whether it be the glorious strands, or the countless little coves this craggy coast hides under its towering cliffs and between its headlands. Like the Phoenicians and Romans before them, they rarely stray from sight of the silky sea in every shade of turquoise blue. But, as alluring as those sands are, it would be a shame to miss the scenery, culture, natural wonders and ancient sites that lie only a few kilometres away in the wild and peaceful interior.

High in the wild and rocky Gennargentu, stone villages cling to steep slopes, and one of Europe's deepest canyons carves its way through this unspoiled mountain range. From late winter through to summer, wildflowers paint the high meadows, and in the autumn the whole island harvests the grapes that produce Sardinia's outstanding wines.

It boggles the mind that more than five millennia ago people figured out how to build multi-storeyed stone towers, 20m (65ft) tall with chambers roofed in unmortared stone, let alone ones with interior staircases tunnelling inside the walls. These complex towers (▷ panel) were so well built that today's visitors can explore their passageways and admire the views from their heights. It is thought they were built first as watchtowers and later as symbols of power to intimidate rivals, and then as defensive strongholds.

History and geography co-operate to scatter Sardinia's highlights—archaeological, artistic and natural—equitably around the island, each region having its own share of must-see places. The happy result of this is that visiting these highlights takes you on a round-island tour, with charming small cities conveniently placed as stopping points along the way.

Facts + Figures

- Sardinia lies 200km (124 miles) north of the African coast and the same distance west of mainland Italy.
- Sardinia is the second-largest island in the Mediterranean after Sicily.
- Sardinia is Italy's largest supplier of cork.

THE MYSTERIOUS NURAGHI

The domes that roof each chamber of the amazing Nuraghic towers are really not true domes. These beehive-shaped vaults, which are formed by concentric layers of huge stones, each extending slightly inward without a keystone, are known as *thalos* domes.

THE LITTLE GREEN TRAIN

The Trenino Verde tourist train crosses some of the island's most inaccessible scenery on narrow-gauge tracks. The route that chugs from Arbatax on the east coast to Mandas in the island's centre is the most scenic, travelling for five hours through the wild mountainous Barbagia region; it is often called the most beautiful rail line in the world.

HERE'S TO A LONG LIFE

Sardinians live longer than people elsewhere in the world, with around 135 locals per million enjoying their 100th birthday party. The average for the western world is about 75 per million. Researchers have collected DNA from communities all over the island to see if they can determine why, but the Sardinians just shrug and say it's the good red wine they drink.

A Short Stay in Sardinia

DAY 1: CÁGLIARI

Morning Begin your day watching local life and boats in the harbour, from a café table under the arcades of Via Roma. Then head up the wide Piazza Carlo Felice to the old **Castello quarter** (▷ 94) to admire the city from Bastione de San Remy or Bastione Santa Croce before climbing the narrow stone-paved streets to visit the Duomo.

Mid-morning Continue uphill, past Palazzo Reggio to Piazza Arsenale, to get a quick lesson in Sardinian prehistory among the amazing collections of ancient bronze, gold and stonework in the **Museo Archeológico** (▷ 95).

Lunch Walk back downhill to Piazza Carlo Felice, to enjoy a sandwich and pastry at **Cafètteria Tiffany** (▷ 106), or explore the streets of the Marina quarter to find a more substantial lunch at one of the many restaurants there.

Afternoon Stroll through the old Stampace quarter to visit the second-century Roman amphitheatre. Catch some late afternoon rays on the sands at **Poetto beach** (▷ 101), and enjoy a cool drink from one of its many *cabanas* before returning to the city (P, PQ, PF buses from Piazza Matteoti).

Dinner Join locals for an aperitif and snacks at **Caffè Libarium** (▷ 105) and watch the sunset from the bastions before strolling down to Via Sardegna to choose from its array of restaurants.

Evening If you enjoy late-night partying, you'll find it at **Jko'** (▷ 105), which opens at midnight. Or dine earlier and take in a concert at **Teatro Lirico** (▷ 105).

DAY 2: ALGHERO

Morning Explore the narrow streets and arch-covered passageways of the old Spanish city as shopkeepers roll up their blinds and Alghero comes to life for the day. Pause to see the cloister and church of **San Francesco**, the baroque church of **San Michele** and the 16th-century cathedral (▷ 24–25).

Mid-morning This city on the Coral Coast is the best place to buy coral jewellery, so take some time to shop, or at least browse in the windows along the narrow cobbled lanes of Via Ferret and Via Roma. Shop for easy-to-carry food souvenirs at **Gustos Ísola dei Sapori** (▷ 38).

Lunch Stop for a custom-made sandwich or bruschetta at one of the inviting cafés on Via Carlo Alberto.

Afternoon Board the *Freccia* or *Attilio Regolo* for a tour to **Grotta di Nettuno** (▷ 28), the magnificent sea caves underneath the cliffs of Capo Caccia. On the way to the caves, the cruise offers the best views of this dramatic promontory and the beaches north of Alghero. If the tour returns in time, take a swim at the beach at **Spiaggia San Giovanni** (▷ 25), just north of the port. When sun begins to drop, watch the sunset from Alghero's walls overlooking the sea, or join locals there in their evening *passeggiata*.

Dinner Dine outside under the arches at **Trattoria Al Refettorio** (▷ 40), or inside in the stone-vaulted dining room. If it is on the menu, try sea anemone.

Evening Catch a visiting band or local jam sessions at **Pocoloco Alghero** (▷ 39).

Top 25

TOP **25**

Alghero ▷ 24–25
Defensive walls separate the old town's tangle of streets from the sea.

Archipélago di La Maddalena ▷ 44–45
Islands protected for their natural environment.

Arzachena ▷ 46–47
Prehistoric remains are dotted in the woods and fields around Arzachena.

Bosa ▷ 26 Pastel buildings climb to the medieval Malaspina Castle, high above the red-tiled rooftops.

Cágliari ▷ 94–95 Walls and bastions rise layer after layer from the Bay of Angels in Sardinia's capital.

Castelsardo ▷ 27 Often called the prettiest town in Italy, especially with the late afternoon sun full upon it.

Costa Smeralda
▷ 48–49 Modern film-star-studded towns carved out of a wilderness shore.

Golfo di Orosei ▷ 80–81 Untouched paradise of hidden beaches and sea caves.

Grotta di Nettuno ▷ 28 Sea-washed caves deep in the rocks of the cliffs.

Ísola Caprera ▷ 50
Garibaldi loved his island home on beautiful, rocky and wild Caprera.

Ísola di Sant'Antíoca/ Ísola di San Pietro ▷ 96
A microcosm of all those who have inhabited or controlled Sardinia.

Ísola Tavolara ▷ 51
Looming Ísola Tavolara's steep cliffs protect birds, goats and other wildlife.

Monti del Gennargentu ▷ 82 Snowcapped in winter, a rugged refuge and the island's tallest mountains.

Nora ▷ 97 A coastal city, the first on the island to be founded by the Phoenicans in the eighth century BC.

Nuraghe Losa ▷ 66–67 Admire the genius of its stone *thalos* domes and interior passageways.

Nuraghe Su Nuraxi ▷ 98 UNESCO World Heritage Site, one of the best restorations in the Mediterranean.

Oristano ▷ 68–69 Oristano retains its regal air as the former capitol of the Kingdom of Arborea.

Santa Cristina Nuraghic Village ▷ 70 A fine specimen, still the scene of an annual pilgrimage.

Santa Teresa di Gallura ▷ 52 Guarding the north coast, the city faces Corsica across the Straits of Bonifacio.

Sássari ▷ 29 Sardinia's second-largest city has remained a centre of learning and culture since the early Renaissance.

Témpio Pausánia ▷ 53 Narrow medieval streets and granite homes appear to be carved from the land.

Thárros ▷ 71 Since the Stone Age, successive peoples have inhabited this rocky point on the Sínis Peninsula.

Tiscali ▷ 83 A great mystery, this remote mountain chasm was a place of refuge in prehistoric times.

Valle dei Nuraghi
▷ 30–31 An outstanding Nuraghe and tombs carved into a rock cliff 6,000 years ago highlight this wide volcanic valley.

Villasimíus and Costa Rei ▷ 99 Perfect beaches and a marine reserve bring people to this seaside town.

These pages are a quick guide to the Top 25, which are described in more detail later. Here they are listed alphabetically, and the tinted background shows which area they are in.

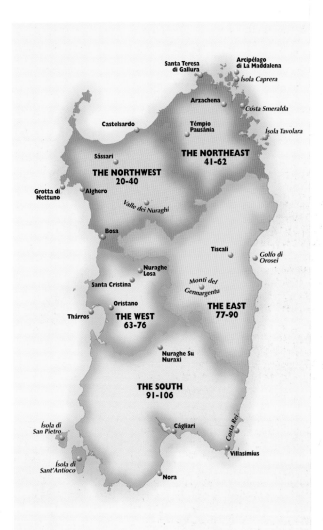

Santa Teresa di Gallura

Arcipélago di La Maddalena

Ísola Caprera

Arzachena

Costa Smeralda

Castelsardo

Témpio Pausánia

Ísola Tavolara

Sássari

THE NORTHEAST
41-62

THE NORTHWEST
20-40

Grotta di Nettuno

Alghero

Valle dei Nuraghi

Bosa

Tiscali

Golfo di Orosei

Nuraghe Losa

Santa Cristina

Monti del Gennargentu

Oristano

THE EAST
77-90

Thárros

THE WEST
63-76

Nuraghe Su Nuraxi

THE SOUTH
91-106

Ísola di San Pietro

Cágliari

Costa Rei

Villasimíus

Ísola di Sant'Antioco

Nora

Out and About

Sardinia is a paradise for travellers who love the great outdoors, offering plenty of options between the glorious coastline and the wild reaches of the inland mountains. The island is dedicated to preserving these open spaces both for recreation and as a habitat for wildlife, which is protected in an astonishing number of parks and reserves where wild ponies, bird species and marine life thrive. In spring, the wildflowers are also spectacular.

Wildlife

Sardinia treasures its wildlife, and reserves protect a number of rare or endangered species. North of Bosa Marina is Italy's only colony of griffon vultures, and it is not uncommon to see them soaring above the precipitous coast. Nearby, stenella dolphin feed on the plentiful fish in the Sea of Sardinia off Alghero, overlooked by the Natural Park of Porto Conte-Capo Caccia where wild Giara ponies are protected. Southwest of Cágliari, above the Costa Sud, the World Wide Fund for Nature protects the indigenous deer, wild boar and birds in the reserve of Monte Arcosu. Wild boar are so common on the island of Caprera that signs warn motorists of *cinghale*. Another offshore island, Tavolara, is part of the Tavolara Marine Reserve, protecting nesting eagles and peregrine falcons, as well as wild goats. The high plateau of Giara di Gesturi, north of Tuili, provides habitat to around 700 small wild horses. The vast lagoon north of Oristano protects not only the abundance of birdlife

BEACHES ARE PUBLIC

All beaches in Sardinia are public and are not owned by the hotels nor by private individuals. Getting to them, however, is sometimes difficult because developers buy the land behind them, effectively cutting off access to anyone but guests at the resort. But if you can figure out a way to get there—by a coastal trail or by boat—you can use any beach on the entire coast.

From top: Explore the Golfo di Orosei by boat; wild boar piglets; gulls thrive on the headlands

ESSENTIAL SARDINIA OUT AND ABOUT

that passes through the wetlands during the spring and fall migrations, but also rare nesting species that are extinct elsewhere in Europe. Flamingos are common here, as are at the protected Stagno di Molentargius, the lagoon behind the Poetta beaches where previously migratory flamingos established nesting grounds in the 1990s.

Weird Rocks

The constant winds sweeping across Sardinia have sculpted the island's rocky landscape into bizarre shapes, especially in the Gallura region, where one high mountain valley is known as Valle della Luna (Valley of the Moon) for its giant otherworldly formations. The same name has been given to a particularly convoluted stretch of granite shapes on Capo Testa, north of Santa Teresa di Gallura, but the name could apply to that entire promontory, so wildly eroded are its rocks.

Wild Landscapes

The vast Parco Nazionale de Golfo di Orosei ensures that great swathes of the undeveloped, and mostly uninhabited, eastern coastline will remain pristine, along with the eastern slopes of the Sopramonte mountain ranges. Between the sea and the highest peaks on the island, the Gola Su Gorruppu is a 6.5km (4-mile) canyon; at 426m (1,499ft) deep, it is Europe's deepest, and the nearby Grotta Ispinigoli cave contains the continent's longest stalagmite, at 38m (125ft).

From top: Stalactites in Grotta Ispinigoli; scuba diving off Pelosa beach; Ísola Tavolara

WATERSPORTS

Scuba diving and snorkelling are popular in several places, including the Arcipélago di La Maddalena (▷ 44) and the entire north coast from the sheltered Gulf of Azenchena to the Gulf of Asinara, where dives reveal reefs, fish and coral. The wildly varying wind directions in the Strait of Bonifacio offer the thrill of a lifetime for experienced sailors, and nearly every coastal town on the entire island has a marina.

Shopping

Sardinia has a legacy of skilled craftsmanship dating back to the Bronze Age, upheld by contemporary artists who work in many of the same media, often using ancient designs as their inspiration. But styles and techniques constantly evolve, which makes shopping for local arts especially exciting.

Metalwork
Sardinian knives are legendary, and the most famous are forged of Damascus steel by blacksmiths in Santu Lussúrgiu, north of Oristano. Far more delicate is the silver filigree jewellery sold all over the island.

Woven Wool and Willow
The coarse fleece of Sardinian sheep is spun and handwoven into thick carpets textured by tight loops that stand up from the surface, often forming patterns in contrasting colours. See them made and buy the best in Aggius, near Témpio Pausánia. Native grasses, woods and reeds provide material for another weaving art, and several towns are especially known for baskets. In Castelsardo and Flussio you'll see them displayed for sale from doorways, where women sit creating them as you watch.

Trees Turned into Art
In the mountains around Dorgali, woodcarvers create the carnival masks used in annual festivities, and carved chestnut wedding chests that can be shipped home. Look for cork crafts around Dorgali and Témpio Pausánia.

JANUARY SALES

January may be Sardinia's rainy season, but, along with water, it rains bargains. Serious bargains–50 per cent off is the starting point, and sales often include a shop's entire stock, to make way for spring styles. Even classics that don't go out of fashion can be scooped up at 50–70 per cent discounts. More sales happen in June, but the big event begins the second week in January.

From top: Torrone *(nougat); local pottery; handmade baskets; market day in Alghero*

Sardinia by Night

Apart from the Costa Smeralda, Sardinia is not a place people flock to for the nightlife. Cágliari, Alghero and Sássari have a more active nightlife than smaller cities, and local hot spots can be found at the popular beach resorts, but they tend to be more in the line of an outdoor dance floor set up beside the beach in the summer.

Late Nights

Sardinians dine late, and think nothing of sitting well into the night with friends over dinner, followed by a leisurely glass of grappa and coffee. People in Cágliari meet for an aperitif at a café, followed by dinner around 9pm and another café stop before moving on to a disco around midnight. In summer, all this changes as locals flee the city for the beaches, and the nightlife goes with them to the many kiosk bars along the Poetto beach or in other summer resorts.

International Glitz

The Costa Smeralda is a world of its own, its international scene the glitziest in Porto Cervo. These resorts rock to their own rhythms, set by the international and yachting crowd. With the exception of one year-round club in Porto Cervo, nightspots close tight in the winter. Not so in Santa Teresa di Gallura, geographically part of the Costa Smeralda but with a more local hum—not as busy as its buzzing summer bar scene, but still lively at weekends all year.

Although Sardinia is not known for its nightlife, there are some chic bars and clubs to be found

NIGHT SHOTS

Avid photographers will want to set up their tripods for night shots of some of Cágliari's architectural highlights, many of which are very well illuminated at night. Lights cast dark shadows that bring out some of the decorative detail of facades such as the Duomo's in sharp relief. Also well lit at night are San Bonaria, the palace and bastions. Or just sit outdoors at a café and enjoy the night views from one of Castello's terraces.

Eating Out

Dining out is a pleasure in Sardinia, whether it's in an innovative Cágliari restaurant or the most modest small-town trattoria. Wherever you eat, your plate (and glass) will almost certainly be filled with wonderful local products.

Dress and Mealtimes

Even in Cágliari, Sardinia is largely a come-as-you-are place. Jackets and ties are not the rule for dining out, although you'll fit in more comfortably in cities in smart casual attire. (Of course in Porto Cervo, you'll only fit in if you are sporting the latest designer wear.) Sardinians dine late, so it is not unusual to find a restaurant deserted at 7.30pm and abuzz at 10pm. Finding a sandwich at lunch may be difficult, since menus are the same for lunch and dinner. It is perfectly acceptable, however, to order only a first course at lunchtime—or only a main at dinner. It's also acceptable to split a main course, tell the waiter *uno per due*. Average restaurant hours are 12–2.30 or 3 and 7.30–10 or 10.30, later in cities.

Trust the *Vino della Casa*

Sardinian wines are excellent, and all local restaurants offer them. In fact, many pride themselves on offering only wines from Sardinian vineyards, usually by the carafe *(vino della casa, house wine)*. If you're uncertain, ask to *prova*—have a taste before ordering a carafe—but you are very likely to be pleased.

SARDINIAN SPECIALITIES

Menus often include these specialities:

Mallareddus—small ridged gnocchi-like pasta often served with tomato sauce and sausage chunks

Culurgiones—fat little pasta filled with potato and cheese

Pane carasau—flat bread

Pane gittau—carasau, brushed with olive oil, sprinkled with sea salt and herbs and re-baked until crisp

Bottarg—dried mullet roe, usually with pasta

Fregula—toasted pasta served in soups

From top: Café terrace at Bastio San Remy, Cágliari; local biscuit eating alfresco, Cágliari marina; bottle of Sardinian wine

Restaurants by Cuisine

Sardinians are fiercely proud of their own cuisine and locally produced ingredients because they are ingrained in their way of life. So restaurants of other ethnicities are rare. For a more detailed description of our recommendations, see Sardinia by Area.

ASIAN

Isaebi (▷ 61)

CREATIVE AND UPDATED LOCAL

Antica Dimora del Gruccione (▷ 76)
Dr. Ampex (▷ 106)
Locanda Il Melograno (▷ 40)
Restaurant Cocco & Dessì (▷ 76)
Ristorante Grillo (▷ 90)
Ristorante Italia (▷ 106)
Su Furraghe Grigliera Pizzeria (▷ 40)
Tenuta Pilastru (▷ 62)
Trattoria Al Refettorio (▷ 40)
Villa Las Tronas (▷ 40)

ENOTECAS AND CAFÉS

Caffè del Mare (▷ 61)
Cafètteria Tiffany (▷ 106)
Enoteca da Liò (▷ 61)

North West Ristorante (▷ 62)
Ristorante Bar Museum (▷ 62)

FISH/SEAFOOD

Da Nardino Ristorante Pizzeria (▷ 61)
I Giardini di Cala Ginepro (▷ 90)
Il Pescatore (▷ 90)
Ristorante da Tonino (▷ 61)
Ristorante Barracuda (▷ 40)
Sa Funta (▷ 76)

FOR MEAT-LOVERS

Al Bue Rosso (▷ 76)
La Bocca del Vulcano (▷ 76)
La Campagnola (▷ 90)
Craf (▷ 76)
Il Maestrale (▷ 62)

TRADITIONAL SARDINIAN

Ai Monti del Gennargentu (▷ 90)
Casa del Vento (▷ 40)
Colibri (▷ 90)
Marina Giò (▷ 106)
Il Naviglio (▷ 76)
Ristorante Albergo Sant'Elene (▷ 90)
Ristorante Don Chisciotte (▷ 90)
Ristorante Gazebo Medioevale (▷ 106)
Ristorante da Maria Giuseppa (▷ 40)
Ristorante Renzo e Rita (▷ 106)
Ristorante Villa di Chiesa (▷ 106)
Su Gologone (▷ 90)
Trattoria La Gallurese (▷ 62)
Trattoria Gennargentu (▷ 106)
Valle dei Vulcani (▷ 40)
Il Vecchio Mulino (▷ 62)

If You Like...

However you'd like to spend your time in Sardinia, these ideas should help you tailor your perfect visit. Each suggestion has a fuller write-up elsewhere in the book.

PREHISTORIC SITES

Climb to the top of Nuraghe Su Nuraxi to appreciate its size (▷ 98).
Marvel at the spiral passageways inside the walls of Nuraghe Losa (▷ 66).
Explore the cave tombs made into homes at Sant'Antíoca (▷ 96).
Look inside the carved tombs at Necropoli di Anghelu Ruju (▷ 32).
Admire the sacred well at Santa Cristina when the morning sun shines down its steps (▷ 70).

Nuraghe Su Nuraxi (above);
Porto Massimo, Ísola La
Maddelena (below)

PERFECT BEACHES

Find a deserted piece of sand to call your own on the Costa Verde (▷ 100).
Join locals on a summer night at the bars along Poetta beach in Cágliari (▷ 101).
Beach-hop by boat in the Maddelena Islands (▷ 44).
Watch the waves roll in along the Costa Rei (▷ 99).
Hike to a beach under the fantastic rock formations on Capo Testa (▷ 52).

KEEPING CHILDREN INTERESTED

Explore stone passageways at Nuraghe Santu Antine and spooky cave-tombs at Sant'Andrea Priu (▷ 31).
Find beaches with a gentle drop-off at Villasimíus and the Costa Rei (▷ 99).
Burn off some energy on the 656 steps of the Escala del Cabirol at the Grotta di Nettuno (▷ 28).
Reach for the stars in the planetarium at Parco Sardegna in Miniatura (▷ 100).
Cool off together on a hot afternoon, at Aquadream Water Park (▷ 55).

Parco Sardegna in
Miniatura, Tuili (bel

COMMUNING WITH NATURE

Join a nature excursion into the Giara di Gesturi to see wild ponies and wildflowers (▷ 101).

Watch eagles and peregrine falcons in the Tavolara Marine Reserve (▷ 51).

Spot Europe's last griffon vultures soaring above the mountains of Bosa Marina (▷ 26).

Explore the wild rocky landscapes of Ísola Caprera on horseback (▷ 50).

Cruise in the Sea of Sardinia to observe stenella dolphins (▷ 39).

SAVOURING LOCAL FLAVOUR

Sample the variety of Galluran specialities at Tenuta Pilastru, in Arzechena (▷ 62).

Tuck into a hearty zuppa Gallura at Trattoria La Gallurese in Témpio Pausánia (▷ 62).

Appreciate the exquisite flavour of *bue rosso* (red ox) in a *carpaccio* at Dr. Ampex in Cágliari (▷ 106).

Have your first taste of sea anemone in Alghero (▷ 24, panel).

*ti del Gennargentu
...ntain range (top); a café
...g the Mirador D'en Camp,
...hero (above)*

PEOPLE-WATCHING

Try to guess who's behind the sunglasses in Porto Cervo's favourite watering holes (▷ 48).

Sit in a café on Cágliari's Bastione Saint Remy at any time of day (▷ 94).

Watch the *passeggiata* on Alghero's walls (▷ 24).

Settle into a café on Piazza Vittorio Emanuele in Santa Teresa di Gallura (▷ 52).

Join the summer evening beach scene at Poetta (▷ 101).

Santa Teresa di Gallura

SPECTACULAR SCENERY

Stand at the point on Capo Testa to view the cliffs of Corsica through fantastic wind-worn rocks (▷ 52).

Scan the mountain horizon south of Arzachena (▷ 46).

Explore the wild and protected coast south of Cala Gonone (▷ 80).

Drive south from Pula to see the promontories and islands of the Costa del Sud (▷ 100).

See the sea from the winding coastal road between Bosa and Alghero (▷ 37).

Tree-lined shore bordering Cala Gonone (above); walkin in Gola Su Gorruppu (below)

ACTIVE SPORTS

Descend by ropes into the 426m (1,397ft) deep canyon floor of Gola Su Gorruppu (▷ 85).

Challenge the winds of the Straits of Bonifacio, off Santa Teresa di Gallura (▷ 52).

Dive to the World War II wrecks in the Gulf of Orosei (▷ 89).

Learn windsurfing in the sheltered cove of Bosa Marina (▷ 26).

Snorkel to see fish in the clear waters off Villasimíus (▷ 99).

A display of local craftsmanship (below)

SERIOUS SHOPPING

Renew your wardrobe in January, when the stores have their biggest and best sales (▷ 12, panel).

Admire the artistry of the island's contemporary craftsmen at Su Gologone (▷ 89).

Look for ISOLA shops in several cities, to discover high-quality handmade gifts. (▷ 89).

Marvel at the beautiful hand-woven carpets at the Aggese Carpet Exhibition in Aggius (▷ 54, 60).

Sample the multitude of Sardinian cheeses before you buy, at straight-from-the-farm prices, at the San Benedetto market (▷ 104).

Sardinia by Area

Soaring headlands end abruptly in cliffs carved with sea caves; pine woods hide white sand; castles crown the streets of medieval towns. Add Romanesque churches, a charming Spanish city, a breathtaking coastal drive, and how could anyone fail to fall in love with Sardinia's northwest?

Alghero

HIGHLIGHTS

● The baroque church of San Michele
● San Francesco cloister
● Walking the walls

TIPS

● The local culinary delicacies are sea anemone and sea urchins, the latter only available in the winter.
● Watch the sunset from the terrace of Villa las Tronas, over a glass of local Malvasia.

Take an evening *passeggiata* among the cafés along the tree-lined terraces of the *bastioni*, the defensive walls that separate Alghero's delightful tangle of stone-paved streets from the sea.

A bit of Spain in Italy When the Pope gave Sardinia to the King of Aragon in the 14th century, inviting the Spanish to take over the island from Pisan-Genovese control, Alghero became their base. Removing the locals almost entirely, the Spanish transported 400 families from Aragon and Catalonia, presenting them with fiefdoms if they would settle the island. The influence lingers today, in street names, cuisine and in the church of San Francesco, where mass is still said in Catalan. Inside, look for the entrance to the sacristy on the left side of the

Clockwise from far left: Towers hyphenate the town's fortifications; columns fronting the Duomo di Santa Maria; a view south from the old town battlements; boats moored at the harbour; the cloister of Chiesa di San Francesco

main altar, for access to the beautiful stone cloister, parts of which date from the 13th century.

City of towers Upper storeys of the old buildings connect across arches that span the streets. You'll eventually find yourself at one of the towers that stud the *bastione*, from which there are views of the sea, Capo Caccia and the city's church towers. Most noticeable of these is San Michele, a baroque Jesuit church, and the Duomo, Alghero's 16th-century cathedral.

The colour of coral This part of Sardinia is known as the Coral Coast, and coral jewellery is displayed in shop windows along the cobbled lanes that wind through Alghero's old city. Sandy beaches extend into the city; the nearest is Spiaggia San Giovanni, north of the port.

THE BASICS

🚌 B5
✉ 11km (7 miles) southeast of Alghero-Fertilia Airport
🛈 Piazza Porta Terra 9, tel 079 979 054,
🍴 Plentiful restaurants and cafés
🚌 From Alghero-Fertilia Airport (20 mins)
♿ Few

Bosa

Cyclist's view from the Ponte Vecchio (left); the castle looms high above the town (right)

THE BASICS

www.bosaonline.com

➕ C7

✉ 45km (27 miles) south of Alghero

🍴 Restaurants and cafés in town and at Bosa marina beach

🚌 From Alghero (55 mins); tourist train from Piazza Monumento to major sights in summer

Castello Malaspina

✉ Sa Costa

☎ 333 544 5675

🕐 Apr–Jun, Sep–Oct daily 10–1, 3.30–6; Jul 10–1, 4–7.30; Aug 10–7.30; Oct–Mar Sat–Sun 10–1, 3.30–6

💰 Inexpensive

San Pietro ex Muras

✉ 2km (1.2 miles) east of Ponte Vecchio

☎ 333 544 5675

🕐 Mar–Oct Tue–Thu 10–12, Fri–Sat 10–12.30, 4–7, Sun 4–7

HIGHLIGHTS

● Malaspina Castle and chapel
● San Pietro ex Muras
● Strolling the esplanade and medieval hill quarter
● Visiting artists' studios and galleries

Pastel buildings line the riverfront and climb in a tangle of medieval lanes to the hilltop Malaspina Castle, from which views extend across tiled rooftops from the fertile valley farmlands to the sea.

City of artists Founded by Phoenicians in the ninth century BC, Bosa thrived as a Roman market town and later port, owing to its location astride the island's only navigable river. The old quarter's charming architecture dates back to the late Middle Ages. The signorial manor Casa Deriu is restored as a museum with a gallery of paintings, ceramics and graphics by native artist Melkiorre Melis. Bosa's unique colours and light have long attracted artists, whose work is seen in Pinacoteca Atza and in the open studios of contemporary artists, both representational and abstract.

Churches Inside the castle walls is a 13th-century chapel, where in 1972 a remarkable 14th-century fresco cycle was discovered. Across the River Temo, the Romanesque San Pietro ex Muras was originally Bosa's cathedral, replaced when the village moved nearer the sea.

Place to relax Stroll the palm-shaded riverside esplanade for views of fishing boats, the graceful Ponte Vecchio and the row of uniform old leather factories across the river, some derelict and others now artists' studios. At the mouth of the Temo, Bosa Marina's beach circles a protected cove overlooked by an Aragonese tower.

The rugged coastline (left); looking up at the imposing ramparts (middle, right)

Castelsardo

Few views in all Italy beat that of the setting sun's rosy light bathing Castelsardo's castle and pale-hued buildings that tumble down the rocky prominence to the sea below it.

Medieval ramparts Castelsardo is crowned not only by a well-preserved 12th-century castle, but by an entire old town of narrow streets that wind down steeply, breaking into steep steps. Inside the castle—from whose ramparts there are views of the north coast and the island of Corsica—is a museum of the local craft of basket-making. Along with baskets to mould the local cheeses and for various other household uses are woven traps for seafood and boats made of reeds, very reminiscent of those made by the Egyptians and those still in use on Bolivia's Lake Titicaca.

Lighthouse to church tower Continue down to Piazza Misericordia and the church of Santa Maria, with a painted and gold pulpit and a side altar with good painted panels. Even farther below is the Duomo, with one of the finest retables in Sardinia, dating from the 15th century; its bell tower was originally a lighthouse.

Exquisite The art of basket-making is well documented in Castelsardo's museum, but it's no match for watching a delicate coiled basket take shape in the hands of an artist. For the best of them, look up the steps beside Via Vittorio Emanuele 24 for a small display.

THE BASICS

🔢 D3

✉️ 32km (20 miles) northeast of Sássari

☎️ Castello Museum: 079 471 380

🕐 Castello Museum: Apr–Oct 9–1, 2–4; Nov–Mar 9.30–1, 3–5.30. Duomo crypt: Mon–Sat 10–1, 3–8

🍴 Restaurants and cafés

🚌 Regular service from Sássari (one hour)

♿ Castello Museum: inexpensive

HIGHLIGHTS

● Viewing the city from the Sássari road at sunset
● Exploring the old streets around the castle
● Shopping for baskets and needlework

Grotta di Nettuno

TOP 25

The vertiginous descent to the cave system (left); inside the stunning grotto (right)

THE BASICS

🚉 B5
✉ Capo Caccia, 24km (14.5 miles) west of Alghero
☎ 079 979 054
🕐 Apr–Sep daily 9–7; Oct 9–6; Nov–Mar 10–1
🍴 Restaurant (€€)
🚌 From the main terminal at Alghero
⛴ Excursions from Alghero
☎ 079 975 213
♿ None
💰 Expensive
❓ Anyone with vertigo should avoid the steep stairs to the grotto carved into the face of the cliff

HIGHLIGHTS

● Stalagmites and stalactites
● Scary stairs
● Towering cliffs of Capo Caccia
● Approaching the cape by boat

Deep within the walls of the massive headland cliffs of Capo Caccia, the sea has worked for millennia to carve a cave system deep into the rock. Inside, a wonderland of stalagmites and stalactites reflect in an underground lake.

Spectacular setting The cliffs of the Capo Caccia tower more than 300m (984ft) over the water, dwarfing the huge lighthouse perched on top of the point. Whether by car or by boat, the approach to Capo Caccia is dramatic. Even more dramatic is the approach to the mouth of the cave itself, whose entrance is at sea level beneath the towering cliff.

The tour The grotto has been carved by the action of the sea over millennia and extends 2,500m (8,200ft) into the huge cliffs of the headland. Inside, a guide leads visitors through a forest of stalagmites and stalactites and around an underground lake. Stunning lighting effects in greens, blues, white and yellows enhance the experience. The tour takes about 45 minutes.

Quite a workout Anyone in top shape—and with a head for heights—can use the Escala del Cabirol (goat stairs), 656 steps that were carved into the sheer cliffs in the 1950s to provide land access to the grotto. A less terrifying experience is to take a boat to the entrance of the cave; a service operates from a small cove nearby on the cape and from Alghero (not in winter).

From left; Santa Maria church; a quiet street; carving on the Duomo; Rosello Fountain

TOP 25

Sássari

Sardinia's second-largest city, a centre of learning and culture since the early Renaissance, has a thriving student life that enlivens its Catalan Gothic, baroque and neoclassical streets with cafés, bars and trendy shops.

Spanish *palazzi* Corso Vittorio Emanuele II was the central street of the medieval city, and is lined by fine old homes from the Spanish period. Some are restored, others look every year of their five centuries, but their old porticos and windows add grace to the *corso*. Scattered between them are the neoclassical Teatro Civico and baroque church of Sant'Andrea.

Dazzling Duomo Narrow curving streets form a spider's web around the *corso*, still the core of the sloping old town. Best known among Sássari's wealth of architecture is the Duomo, whose amazing carved facade uses every cliché in the language of 17th-century stonework. Milanese artisans carved its swirling arabesques and it flourishes in intricate detail. Off Piazza Mercado is the monumental Renaissance fountain Fonte di Rosello, built in marble by Genoese workers.

Beautiful beaches Don't ignore the idyllic dune-backed beaches of white sand and gentle waves that lie north of the city, extending along the Golfo dell'Asinara to Castlesardo. Low pine forests border the shore, the carpet of green broken by regular paths from the coastal road.

THE BASICS

🔶 C4

✉ 30km (18 miles) east of Alghero-Fertilia Airport

🍽 Abundant restaurants and cafés

🚆 Regular service from Cágliari

🚌 Regular service from Cágliari

❓ Large car park between Corso Vittorio Emanuele II and the Duomo

HIGHLIGHTS

● Museo Nazionale Sanna (▷ 35)
● The Duomo
● Strolling Corso Vittorio Emanuele II
● Golfo dell'Asinara beaches

THE NORTHWEST

★

TOP 25

Valle dei Nuraghi

HIGHLIGHTS

● Nuraghe Santu Antine
● Sant'Andrea Priu
● Medieval village at Rebeccu
● Museo Archeológico at Torralba

TIP

● Sant'Andrea Priu hours are irregular; call ahead for an appointment ☎ 348 564 2611. If the gate is closed, drive past and go through the fence opening for a sheep path to cliff-top tombs.

Tombs carved into a rock cliff 6,000 years ago and one of the island's three best Nuraghic towers top the list of prehistoric sites in this wide volcanic valley.

Valley of volcanoes The flat valley is surrounded by hills of wildly eroded boulders, and dotted by the perfect cones of ancient volcanoes. Scattered across this landscape are several Nuraghi. The largest and most complex is Nuraghe Santu Antine, its three towers, built in the 16th century BC, connected by a bastion. The entrance leads into a large courtyard, from which passages lead around the towers. The central tower has three levels, its first and second floors intact, along with the floor and some walls of a third level, which originally reached 25m (82ft), all of dry stone construction. To

Clockwise from far left: A cone tower in the shape of a beehive, Santu Antine; corridor in Santu Antine; looking down over the prehistoric remains at Santu Antine; other prehistoric remains scattered across the valley

the left of the tower entrance a winding staircase leads inside the wall to the upper level, and from the top are splendid views. From the west tower an upper corridor leads to the north tower. All this makes Santu Antine one of the most interesting Nuraghi to explore.

Prehistoric tombs A short drive away, Sant'Andrea Priu is a complex of tombs carved into a rock face. Called *domus de janas* in Sardinia, these date from 4000–3000BC and were used in medieval times as chapels and hermitages. Some larger, interconnected rooms still show frescoes painted during later Christian use. At the top are more, smaller tombs and a huge rock carved to represent (it is thought) a bull. In Torralba, the Museo Archeológico has excavated items from the Valle dei Nuraghi.

THE BASICS

www.nuraghesantuantine.it
🔢 D6
✉ Off SS131, Torralba
☎ 079 847 298 or 079 847 145; Museo Archeológico 079 847 296
🕐 Apr–Oct daily 9–6; Nov–Mar 9.30–12.30, 3–6
🍴 Café at entrance (€)
🚌 From Sássari to Torralba
♿ None
💶 Inexpensive (includes admission to Museo Archeológico)

More to See

FLUSSIO

www.comune.flussio.nu.it

In the highlands near Bosa, and on that city's 'Strada della Malvasia' wine route, Flussio and its neighbouring village of Tinnura are known for their baskets. Driving along the SS292, which runs through the middle of both towns, is like driving through a bazaar, with baskets displayed on the roadsides in front of houses. Asphodel, reed and willow all grow locally, and are the primary materials for both woven and coil baskets. The cut plants can be seen laid out to dry in the sun. Traditionally, women have made the more decorative coiled baskets, while men made the woven baskets used for farming.

🔶 C7 ✉ West of Bosa 🍴 Several in town 🚌 From Sássari ♿ Few

ÍSOLA ASINARA

www.parcoasinara.org

The Romans called it the Island of Hercules but today it is named for the small herd of *asinara* (wild donkeys) that share it with *cinghiale* (wild pigs) and *mouflon* (wild sheep). Until the late 19th century a few shepherding families lived here, but they were deported to the main island so the Italian government could establish a quarantine station and later a prison. Now the beautiful wild Parco Nazionale di Asinara, it has no human population and permission is required to visit. Authorized boats, bicycle rental and scuba diving operators, with contact data, are listed on its website. Boats to the island depart from Porto Tórres or the nearer Stintino, an attractive town established by families dispossessed from Asinara.

🔶 B2 ✉ Northwest of Porto Tórres ☎ 079 503 388 🕐 By reservation 🚌 From Porto Tórres to Stintino ♿ None 🎫 Free; boat moderate

NECROPOLI DI ANGHELU RUIU

One of Sardinia's most important ancient sites, this field of 38 tombs carved into the sandstone and

The shores of Ísola Asinara lapped by waters in every shade of blue

used for burials between 3000 and 1500BC is astonishing for both its size and its complexity. Two types of tombs were carved out of the soft rock with primitive stone picks, the oldest irregular in shape, following the sandstone deposits. The later tombs are more consistent in shape, forming a T or with several tombs opening onto a central space. Some have architectural features, including doorframes, false doors, carved steps and pillars. Carry an electric torch to see the extensive interiors and carvings of bulls' heads in bas relief above doorways, but be prepared to crouch, as the ceilings are very low. Some of the lower tombs may be flooded by winter rains, but there is plenty to see here without going inside them.

➕ B5 ✉ SP42 at Olmedo, 9km (5.5 miles) north of Algherio ☎ 079 989 7502
🕐 Nov–Feb daily 10–2; Mar 9.30–4; Apr–Oct 9–7 ♿ Pathways are relatively smooth and level for exterior views
👆 Inexpensive

NURAGHE APPIU

Although the Nuraghic tower itself is unrestored and not one of the most impressive, the complex is one of the island's most interesting. Prepare to walk across pastures and on woodland trails, through a beautiful landscape high above the coast to see menhirs, a 'giant's tomb' (megalithic corridor grave), a small Nuraghe and one of Sardinia's largest Nuraghic villages of some 200 huts surrounding the main tower. Excavations of the tower itself began in 2010. The village contains several unusual features, including hearths, niches, a stone tub and a drainage pipe.

➕ C6 ✉ Unnumbered paved road signposted from SP49, or from S292 in Villanova Monteleone ☎ 079 960 607
🕐 Summer 9.30–7.30; winter 9.30–5.30
🍴 Café at entrance, erratic hours (€)

NURAGHE DI PALMAVERA

The small Nuraghe is particularly interesting for the visible building phases, clear because the stone

The prehistoric village of Nuraghe di Palmavera

used changed from limestone in the 10th–15th-century BC tower and first huts to reddish sandstone in the later ninth-century reinforcements of the central tower and construction of the second tower and the Reunion Hut. In the eighth century, limestone was used again to partially reconstruct the second tower, huts and outer wall. At the end of the eighth century, the village was destroyed by fire. In the centre of the round Reunion Hut is a reproduction of the original carved stone miniature of a complete Nuraghe, which first allowed archaeologists to understand what the original tower tops looked like.

➕ B5 ✉ SS127, Alghero (on road to Capo Caccia) ☎ 329 438 5947
🕐 Nov–Feb daily 10–2; Mar 9.30–4; Apr–Oct 9–7 🚌 From Alghero to Capo Caccia pass the site ♿ Few
💷 Inexpensive

PORTO TÓRRES

The Romanesque Basilica of San Gavino was built in the 11th and 12th centuries, and its crypt created in the early 17th century after the discovery of the relics of three early Christian martyrs, Gavino, Proto and Gianuario. Inside the church, the three are also commemorated by an unusual triple monument with reclining polychrome wooden statues. Near the ferry port in Porto Tórres are first-century Roman sites, including a bridge and baths.

➕ C4 ✉ 20km (12 miles) northwest of Sássari 🍴 Nearby restaurants and cafés
🚌 From Sássari ♿ None 💷 Free

ROCCIA DELL'ELEFANTE

A huge limestone outcrop has been eroded by wind and rain into the shape of an elephant, its trunk overhanging a small road above the N134. Tombs have been carved into its base by prehistoric people, turning a natural curiosity into a prehistoric site.

➕ D3 ✉ San Giovanni, just off N134, southeast of Castelsardo ♿ None, but visible from road 💷 Free

San Gavino Basilica, Porto Tórres

Roccia dell'Elefante

SANTISSIMA TRINITÀ DE SACCARGIA BASILICA

In the middle of sheep pastures, the striking black-and-white-striped Romanesque church, with a tall square tower, rises out of the valley, flanked by the remaining arcades of its ruined cloister. Inside are medieval frescoes from the 12th century. The complex was originally a Benedictine monastery.

➕ D5 ✉ SS131, 13km (8 miles) south of Sássari ☀ Apr–Oct (hours vary) 🍴 Café at site (€) ♿ None; exterior fully visible 💵 Free

SÁSSARI: MUSEO NAZIONALE SANNA

www.museosannasassari.it

One of the most important museums in Sardinia, Museo Sanna's collections are classified into archaeology, ethnology and paintings. Its archaeological collections, derived from excavations and study of tombs, include works from the Nuraghic through the Aragonese period and are noted in particular for Nuraghic bronze figures, pottery and jewellery. New exhibit rooms concentrate on the findings at the temple at nearby Monti d'Accoddi and the Roman period.

➕ C4 ✉ Via Roma 64 ☎ 079 272 203 ☀ Tue–Sun 9–8 🍴 Several nearby ♿ Very good 💵 Inexpensive

SPIAGGIA DELLA PELOSA

Once among the finest stretches of sand in Sardinia, this coast has been seriously damaged by the sea, greatly diminishing its beaches. Close-packed development encrusts the hillside behind the promenade where the beaches were. The pretty town of Stintino, clustered in pastel cubes around its little harbour, is the departure point for boats to Ísola Asinara (▷ 32), and to its south are the long beaches of Spiaggia Saline, also eroded.

➕ B3 ✉ Stintino, 28km (17 miles) north-west of Porto Tórres 🍴 Several in Stintino 🚌 To beaches from Stintino ♿ Few 💵 Free; parking in summer inexpensive

White sands and clear water at Spiaggia della Pelosa

Santissima Trinità de Saccargia

Bosa to Alghero

Great views, rocky points with Spanish towers, beaches, craggy cliffs and prehistoric sites make this a beautiful and varied route.

DISTANCE: 63km (39 miles)   **ALLOW:** 4 hours with stops

START

BOSA
➕ C7

1 Leave Bosa (▷ 26) on Via Alghero, turning left across the river to Bosa Marina. Turn right to explore its waterfront and beach. Return to the bridge, going straight ahead on the SP49.

2 After reaching the top of the headland, watch for the lane heading left to the small beach of Cala S'Abba Druche.

3 Continue north, under a rocky ridge, with ever-changing sea, to a small car park on the left at Casa del Vento, a good stop for lunch on the terrace (▷ 40).

4 Follow the coast road as it climbs another headland, descending for spectacular views. Turn right on the road marked 'Nuraghe Appiu'.

END

ALGHERO
➕ B5

8 In a cove sheltered by the rocky point of Torre Poglina is the beach of Spiaggia de Poglina, with a café and parking. Continue north through orange groves to the walled city of Alghero (▷ 24).

7 On reaching the SP49 again, turn right to follow the rocky coast, where views now include the city of Alghero and beyond it the cliffs at Capo Caccia.

6 Leave Nuraghe Appiu, retracing the route through high pastures of sheep and cattle, with a completely different set of views—some from the top of a knife-edge ridge with sea views below on both sides.

5 The road climbs steeply to a high plateau to reach the prehistoric complex of Nuraghe Appiu (▷ 33).

Shopping

ARADENA

An interesting little store selling the arts, flavours and traditional crafts of Sardinia, including the legendary handmade knives.

b5 ✉ Via Gioberti 24–28, Alghero ☎ 079 973 5058

ARTIGIANATO DI MARRAS M. ANGELA

Beautiful hand-embroidered rugs, bedspreads and table linens are made by Marras Angela, who will demonstrate this unusual local technique for you. Baskets and ceramics by local artisans are all well above the standard of items found in the tourist *artigianato* shops.

D3 ✉ Via Roma 50, Castelsardo ☎ 079 471 266

ARTIGIANATO TIPICO SARDO

Sardinian handicrafts and souvenirs, including coral jewellery and handmade knives forged of Damascus steel.

b5 ✉ Via Roma 24, Alghero ☎ 079 975 534

LA BOTTEGA

A splendid small shop filled with all sorts of Sardinian fare. They have a good variety of cheeses, *bottarga* (dried mullet roe), sweets and pastas, as well as traditional breads. They are happy to ship your purchases if you prefer.

D3 ✉ Via Trento 1B, Castelsardo ☎ 079 471 024

LA BOTTEGA

www.labottegasarda.com
Since 1978 La Bottega has been a source of typical Sardinian food products, such as artisanal cheeses, salami, dried pastas, olive oil, *torrone*, biscuits and an excellent wine selection.

C4 ✉ Piazza XX Settembre 1, Porto Tórres ☎ 079 514 834

ESEDRA SARDEGNA

Fine Sardinian handicrafts and design, including filigree jewellery, ceramics and beautiful Christmas nativity figures.

C7 ✉ Corso Vittorio Emanuele 64, Bosa ☎ 0785 374 258

GIOIELLERIA MURA

The stylish shop features jewellery in silver, gold and precious stones, plus gifts, decorative arts, a few antiques and some fine art.

C4 ✉ Via Roma 12, Sássari ☎ 079 235 332

GUSTOS ÍSOLA DEI SAPORI

A good source of high-quality authentic Sardinian food specialities, this shop features traditional sweets, pastas, olive oils, liqueurs, cheese and cured meats at fair prices. The English-speaking owner is very knowledgeable about local foods, and offers samples.

b5 ✉ Via Machin 33 (corner Via Barceloneta), Alghero ☎ 079 994 6031

NAÍTANA

Handicraft shop specializing in high-quality artisanal sandals and belts. They also repair fine leather goods.

b5 ✉ Via Machin 26, Alghero ☎ 079 975 954

SELLA AND MOSCA VINEYARDS

www.sellaemosca.com
These vineyards are one of the finest on the island, with more than 500ha (1235 acres) in production. During a visit here, there is the opportunity to taste the top-quality wines before you make your purchase.

B5 ✉ 10km (6 miles) north of Alghero on the road to Porto Tórres ☎ 079 997 700 ⏰ Jun to mid-Oct, Mon–Sat

---

BASKET TRADITION

Asphodel, reed and willow grow throughout north-western Sardinia. Both Castelsardo and Flussio are known for their long tradition of basket-making. The art and its history are illustrated in Castelsardo's museum, where reed boats, shellfish traps and other uses are shown as well. Baskets are used in a variety of ways, including to mould cheese. The intricate designs that appear to be stamped on aged cheese are actually the imprints of the baskets they were formed in.

Entertainment and Activities

AGRITURISMO MARTE PIRAS
Horse riding lessons and trail rides are available to guests and the public.
➕ C7 ✉ Road between Porto Alabe and Tresnuraghes, south of Bosa Marina ☎ 0785 359 275 ⏲ By reservation only

BATRAKOS DIVING
www.batrakosdiving.it
Batrakos is a fully PADI-qualified operator with 16 different dives on offer, including a dive to a wreck. Most of the dives are in the Gulf of Asinara and include reefs, fish and coral.
➕ D3 ✉ Corso Italia 46, Castelsardo ☎ 079 474 586 ⏲ By reservation only

BOSA DIVING CENTRE
Scuba diving courses with PADI-qualified instructors along the west coast. Also, you can rent rafts for day trips.
➕ C7 ✉ Viale Colombo, Bosa Marina ☎ 0785 375 649

DIVING MALESH
www.divingmalesh.com
Take a cruise on the River Temo and around the stunning surrounding coast. Diving trips to Grotta Casa del Vento, Grotta dei Saggi and other coastal sites are also offered.
➕ C7 ✉ Embark at Nautica Pinna, Bosa Marina ☎ 328 491 5501 ⏲ May–Oct daily 9.30–1, 3.30–7

DOLPHIN CRUISES
www.grottedinettuno.it
Along with daily excursions to the Grotta di Nettuno, the *Freccia* and *Attilio Regolo* offer short cruises to watch dolphins in the Riviera del Corallo.
➕ b4 ✉ Port of Alghero (Banchina Garibaldi) ☎ 079 975 213

MAJORCA WINE PUB
The small, intimate wine bar-pub serves snacks as well, and is a good place for a drink before or after dinner.
➕ b5 ✉ Via Majorca 7, Alghero ☎ 079 590 9410

MARE NATURA
www.marenatura.it
This multi-service agency can arrange visits and boat tours to the Parco

WILDLIFE WATCHING
The west coast between Bosa and Capo Caccia is rich in wildlife, in the sea, on land and in the air. Bosa is the only place in Italy that still has griffon vultures, and the colony of nearly 100 grows slowly. The stenella dolphin thrives in the waters off the Riviera del Corallo, feeding on the numerous species of fish. The coast takes its name from the red coral found in abundance here. North of Alghero, a Giara wild pony herd is protected in the Natural Park of Porto Conte-Capo Caccia.

dell'Asinara, the island off the north coast (▷ 32).
➕ B3 ✉ Via Sássari 77, Stintino ☎ 079 520 097 ⏲ By reservation only 🚢 From Alghero and Porto Tórres

PARADISE CLUB
Dance under the stars in the summer, at this local favourite.
➕ C7 ✉ On the beach at Turas, south of Bosa Marina ⏲ Daily from 11pm

POCOLOCO ALGHERO
www.pocolocoalghero.it
Features live music with visiting major bands and artists, or local jam sessions. Music of all types including Latin and varied styles of jazz. The internet point is open from 7pm.
➕ b5 ✉ Via Gramsci 8, Alghero ☎ 079 973 1034 ⏲ Daily from 8pm

RENTABIKE RAGGI DI SARDEGNA
Bicycle rentals for use in the area or for longer cycling holidays, as well as a good source of information on routes.
➕ b5 ✉ Via Majorca 119, Alghero ☎ 334 305 2480

WINDSURFING CLUB, BOSA MARINA
You can rent windsurfs and kite-surfs for use in the idyllic sheltered waters of the cove at Bosa Marina
➕ C7 ✉ Bosa Marina beach, opposite La Bussola

THE NORTHWEST ENTERTAINMENT AND ACTIVITIES

Restaurants

CASA DEL VENTO (€–€€)

Casa is situated off the highway from Bosa to Alghero on a cliff overlooking the dramatic west coast. A bit far out of town for dinner, it is perfect for a leisurely lunch. Exceptional *pane fratau*.
➕ C6 ✉ Stra SP49, 7km (4 miles) north of Bosa Marina ☎ 347 182 2074 ⏰ Daily 11.30–3.15, 7.30–11.30

LOCANDA IL MELOGRANO (€€)

www.locandailmelograno.com
The owners (both speak English) are passionate about using the products that grow in the river valley below their hillside restaurant opposite the castle, preparing them in original ways. Family-friendly.
➕ C7 ✉ Località Tiria 1, Bosa ☎ 339 469 7178 ⏰ Apr–Oct dinner daily; Nov–Mar closed Mon

RISTORANTE BARRACUDA (€–€€)

Located close to the river, Barracuda is a rare place open when many others are closed on Mondays. The setting is bright and friendly and the food

good; the pasta with clams is outstanding.
➕ C7 ✉ Via Repubblica 21, Bosa ☎ 0785 373 7719 ⏰ Daily lunch and dinner

RISTORANTE DA MARIA GIUSEPPA (€–€€)

The traditional menu of this small family-run place includes snails prepared in various delectable ways and *pane carasau* (crisp flatbread) with pecorino cheese.
➕ D3 ✉ Via Nazionale 20, Castelsardo ☎ 079 470 661 ⏰ Tue–Sun lunch and dinner

SU FURRAGHE GRIGLIERA PIZZERIA (€–€€)

www.sufurraghe.it
Located in a B&B of the same name, the restaurant prides itself on its

selection of local dishes, especially grilled fish. In summer dining is available on their patio.
➕ C5 ✉ Via Su Furraghe 24, Olmedo ☎ 079 902 308, 348 816 3292 ⏰ Daily lunch and dinner

TRATTORIA AL REFETTORIO (€€)

www.alrefettorio.it
Wine bar restaurant specializing in the cuisine of the Alghero region, updated to a stylish standard that is not pretentious. Look for fried sea anemones, lamb with artichokes and olives, *cinghiale* (wild boar) in sweet-sour sauce, *culurgiones* (filled pasta) with *ragu* of baby Sardinian pig and pecorino cheese. The outdoor café is under an arch over a narrow street.
➕ b5 ✉ Carrero del Porxo (Vicolo Adami) 47, Alghero ☎ 079 973 1126 ⏰ Daily lunch and dinner

VALLE DEI VULCANI (€–€€)

www.valledeivulcani.com
This welcome oasis is located in the middle of the wild volcanic landscapes near the Valle de Nuraghe prehistoric sites. The grilled local sausage is excellent, as are the pastas, which are made right there.
➕ D6 ✉ Località Funtana Puttuddi, Giave ☎ 079 847 480 ⏰ Mar–Dec daily lunch and dinner; Jan–Feb closed Tue, Wed

Only a few kilometres from the emerald sea, white-sand beaches and super-luxe resorts, the Costa Smeralda is justly famed for soaring mountains, centuries-old villages and prehistoric sites.

Santa Teresa di Gallura

Punta Falcone

la Marmorat

Capo Testa
Santa Reparata

133bis

*Pur
dei
Vace*

Porto Pozzo

Cala Vall' Alta
Cala
Pischina

Rena Majore

Capannác

Vignola Mare
l'Agnata

Punta di li Francesi
Portobello
di Gallura

Basscutena

Cala Sarraina

Aglientu

Cuoni

Luogosanto

Costa
Paradiso

G   *a*   *l*   *l*   *u*   *r*

Punta li Canneddi

*Ísola
Rossa*

Ísola
Rossa

Vignola

765
▲
Serra di
lu Tassu

133

*Lago di
Liscia*

Sant'Antonio

Trinità d'Agultu
e Vignola

Carana

427

Badesi

Carana

Valle della Luna

Lúras

Calangiánus

Priatu

913 ▲
Punta Sálici

Ággius

Bortigiádas

**Témpio
Pausánia**

127

Monti Ultu

127

Serra Balascia

Valicciola

1359
▲
Punta
Balestrieri

392

Monti

389

Berchidda

199

d *i* *Alà*

Éleme

*Lago del
Coghinas*

597

Oschiri

Rio Rizolu

Monti

1077
▲
Punta di
Senalonga

926 ▲
Punta
sa Mesa

Alà dei Sardi

Altopian

di Buddus

Budduso

Ísola azzoli
Ísola la Presa
Ísola S. Maria
Ísola Budelli
sola Spargi

Arcipélago di La Maddalena

Ísola Maddalena

La Maddalena

Ísola Caprera

Ísola Santo Stéfano

33

Palau

Punta Rossa
Ísola delle Bisce
Capo Ferro

Báia Sardínia

125

Aquadream
Porto Cervo

Ísola di li Nibani

Cannigíone

419
Monte Moro

Arzachena

Capriccioli

Ísola Mortório

231
Monte Villico

Costa Smeralda

Ísola Soffi

San Pantaleo

Punta della Volpe

427

Punta del Canigione

Golfo Aranci

125

San Giovanni

Capo Figari

Santa Lucia

Ísola di Figarolo
Punta delle Casette

Monti sa Curi

Golfo di Ólbia

Capo Ceraso

Punta Timone

Ólbia

Ísola Tavolara

127

Ólbia-Costa Smeralda

131 dcn

Murta Maria

Riserva Marina Tavolara-Punta Coda Cavallo

Ísola Molara

elti

S. Simone

Aratena

199

Enas

Lóiri

E840

Porto San Paolo

Punta di Levante

125

Capo Coda Cavallo

Monte Petrosu

Berchiddeddu

Andria Puddu

Punta Sabbatino

389

Mamusi

Padru

San Teodoro

Punta d'Ottiolo

Monte Nieddu

Punta li Cucutti

Mannu

Budoni

Ludurru

Punta dell' Asino

125

sos Sonórcolos

G   **H**   **J**

0   10 km
0   5 miles

Arcipélago di La Maddalena

HIGHLIGHTS

● Town of La Maddalena
● Garibaldi's home
● Ísola Caprera
● Boat trips to beaches on uninhabited islands (▷ 60)

TIPS

● From La Maddalena harbour follow 'Panoramica' signs to tour the coast.
● Hiking is over rough ground and sharp rock; use proper footwear.
● Carry food and water to Caprera beaches.

Rocky, wild, isolated and the birthplace of Giuseppe Garibaldi, Italy's national hero, the islands of this archipelago are a place for quiet hikes, enjoying nature and swimming at superb white-sand beaches.

National park Of the seven major islands only La Maddalena, San Stefano and Caprera (▷ 50) are inhabited. The others—Spargi, Santa Maria, Budelli and Razzoli—remain wild, surrounded by smaller islets. Combined, they form the Parco Nazionale dell' Arcipélago di La Maddalena, a protected wildlife area.

Stroll through town Ísola La Maddalena is by far the largest and the most populated and is easily accessed by ferries from Palau. Most of the island's population is concentrated in the

Clockwise from far left: A beautifully maintained, ornate house facade in the town of La Maddalena; the rocky coastline of the archipelago; fishing boats line La Maddalena's harbour front; cyclists pause to admire the view

port city of La Maddalena. West of its ferry port is an attractive little harbour filled with colourful fishing boats and sailboats. Narrow streets radiate into the old town, winding and twisting uphill, and connect to a pleasant little *piazza*. From the heights above the town, Corsica and the Galluran coast and mountains are visible.

Islands in history Caprera is the second largest, connected to La Maddalena by a causeway. At one end, Garibaldi's home is now a national monument, and the rest is wild landscape ringed by sand beaches. San Stefano, opposite La Maddalena, was until recently an American submarine base, now being developed as a resort. Admiral Nelson considered the Maddalenas strategically important and spent more than a year here with his fleet before heading off to Trafalgar.

THE BASICS

➕ G1
✉ Off the north coast opposite Palau
🍴 Plentiful in La Maddalena
🚌 Services reach most beaches as far as Trinity Bay
🚢 Saremar Ferry (☎ 0789 737 660; www.saremar.it); Delcomar Ferry (☎ 0789 739 088, 0781 857 123; www.delcomar.it). Tickets at the port, frequent departures
♿ Good
🆓 Free

Arzachena

TOP 25

HIGHLIGHTS

- Coddu Vecchiu
- Li Lolghi
- Necropolis of Li Muri
- Nuraghe Albucciu

TIP

- Pick up the useful route map of sites available at the Tourist office on the SS125.

With one of Sardinia's highest concentrations of sites from the Stone and Copper Ages, this former farming town adds substance to the Costa Smeralda's touristic glitz.

Unlike its neighbours Although it's called the 'Capital of the Costa Smeralda', Arzachena could hardly have less in common with those made-for-tourist coastal enclaves. Steep streets end in long stairways, one of which reaches the Chiesa Santa Lucia and a small museum of local life. East of the centre stands 'Il Fungo', a huge mushroom-shaped rock.

Giants' graves Outstanding prehistoric sites surround Arzachena, including two *tomba gigante* (chambered tombs). Coddu Vecchiu

The distinctive mushroom-shaped rock, Roccia Il Fungo (top left and right); a view over the giants' tomb at Coddu Vecchiu (bottom right); standing stones mark the giants' tomb at Li Lolghi (bottom left)

began as a tunnel grave c.18th century BC, with a semicircular facade added in the 16th to 12th centuries BC. Atop a wooded hill another giants' tomb, Li Lolghi, is similar, with a central stele (standing stone) 3.75m (12.5ft) tall. At its base a small opening leads into the tomb, which has two chambers. Nearby is the necropolis of Li Muri, where stone graves were built in circles of flat standing stones thought to have originally held earth mounds covering the tombs.

Arzachena's Nuraghi Unlike the usual round towers, Nuraghe Albucciu is ovoid, one side built into a large stone outcrop that forms a terrace above it. Evidence shows its use as a fortified residence. Nuraghe La Prisgiona and the Nuraghic complex of Malchittu demonstrate more variations.

THE BASICS

www.arzachena-costasmeralda.it

🔀 G2–3

✉ 26km (16 miles) north of Ólbia

☎ 0789 844 055

🕓 Except Nuraghe, entrance gates are left open when ticket kiosk is closed

🍴 Plentiful in Arzachena

🚌 Frequent service from Ólbia

♿ Few

💰 Free–moderate; combined ticket for all sites

Costa Smeralda

HIGHLIGHTS

- Yacht harbour at Porto Cervo
- Capo Ferro
- Golfo di Arzachena
- Parco Nazionale dell' Arcipélago di La Maddalena
- Capo Testa

TIP

- Báia Sardinia (▷ 55), northwest of Porto Cervo, is a bit less pretentious and lower-key, set on a beautiful crescent white-sand beach.

Smart and made for the moneyed, the Costa Smeralda is where the glitterati hang out amid pink villas and luxurious hotels; this is a place for celebrity-spotting day and night.

Jet-set enclave Perched in the northeast of the island, the Emerald Coast stretches from just north of Ólbia to Capo Testa, a section of rocky coasts interspersed with sandy beaches, stretches of *macchia* and holiday complexes. Porto Cervo, the largest development of the Costa Smeralda, was where the Aga Khan created this refuge for the very wealthy in the 1960s. Built in a rusticated Mediterranean style, with sponged walls in deep colours, of which terracotta predominates on the waterfront, it is designed to be a cute approximation of a

Idyllic whitewashed villas are dotted about the Costa Smeralda (left); the blue-green waters of the Costa Smeralda sparkling like a jewel (right)

fishing village. A little footbridge connects to a 'village' of arcades and streets, linking the resorts to the designer-label shops and mega-yachts in the small harbour. It has all the usual suspects for a celebrity watering hole, most lively in the summer when the stars are out.

Beyond Porto Cervo Other towns of note along the coast are Liscia di Vacca, Capriccioli, Cala di Volpe, Cugnana and Marina di Portisco, and all are favoured as summer resorts by the rich and famous. Another, Porto Rotondo, is known as the 'Venice of Sardinia'. The round arches, pastel stucco walls and mellow-Med architecture are very similar from town to town, high-end villas and luxury hotels flowing gently down sloping hillsides to the turquoise sea, often with a small yacht harbour nearby.

THE BASICS

www.portocervo.net
✚ H3
✉ North of Ólbia
🍴 Plentiful in all towns
🚌 Resorts often offer shuttles to beaches
⛴ Ferry at Palau for La Maddelena Archipelago
♿ Good

Ísola Caprera

Cool white buildings of the Museo Garibaldi (left, middle); sailing off the island's shores (right)

THE BASICS

www.compendiogaribaldino.it

🌐 G2

✉ La Maddalena Archipelago, north of Palau

☎ 0789 727 162

🕐 Tue–Sat 9–1.30, 2–6.30, Sun 9–1.30

🍴 Tiny bar at entrance (€)

🚌 From La Maddalena to Garibaldi house and beaches

⛴ Ferry from Palau to La Maddalena

♿ Few

💶 Garibaldi house: moderate

❓ Garibaldi house by guided tours only

HIGHLIGHTS

● Garibaldi House
● Turquoise sea
● Pink beach at Punta Rosa
● Signs warning drivers to beware of wild boar

It's easy to see why Italy's national hero was glad to get back to his home on Caprera: beautiful, rocky and wild, a good place for walking and for swimming in the turquoise waters from tiny beaches.

Father of the Italian state The second largest island in the archipelago, Caprera is connected to La Maddalena by a causeway and bridge. Its only road leads to the home Garibaldi left to lead the fight for Italian unity and where he returned to farm when his fight had ended. His home is a national monument, almost a shrine for Italians. He bought half of the island in 1855; the remainder was presented to him later by admirers. The simple white-stucco home tells his tale with the tools he used, his clothing and weapons, his wheelchairs, sextants, portraits and photos and his famed red shirt. In later years he described himself as a farmer and fisherman, living his last 26 years here, and died in an elevated bed so that he could look out over his gardens to the sea.

Pink sand, turquoise water In the other direction, the road leads through pines and olive trees to the small Museo Geologico-Mineralogico and on through fragrant *macchia* and eroded rocks to a series of beaches. Few are marked, but they can be spotted by the paths leading to them. The metalled road ends at a wide beach and causeway to Punta Rosa, the island's southernmost point, named for its red granite, which colours the sands pink.

Starfish thrive among the coral (left); the island rising out of the sea (right)

Ísola Tavolara

Several kilometres off the coast, this tiny island's height dominates the resort town of Porto San Paolo. Even on a misty day it's an impressive sight, an immense grey shape like a mystical apparition.

Peninsula Only 1km (0.6 miles) wide by 6km (4 miles) long, the island has sheer cliff sides at an altitude of 564m (1,850ft). There is evidence of human occupation during the Paleolithic era, when it was joined to the mainland. About 10,000 years ago the land connecting it eroded. It has been occupied by shepherds, pirates, fishermen and the military; part of the island is still a military zone.

Smallest kingdom In 1833 Carlo Alberto, king of Piedmont and Sardinia, paid a visit to the island to hunt the wild goats that inhabit its highlands. The island's owner, Giuseppe Bertoleoni, showered great hospitality on the king, so much so that upon departing the king crowned Giuseppe king of Tavolara, making it one of the smallest kingdoms in Europe. The present king, Carlo II, also bears the more common name of Tonini Bertoleoni and operates the Da Tonino restaurant on the island.

Wildlife The island is almost deserted in winter and is part of a protected marine reserve. It attracts many wildlife-watchers, who come to see the rare birds that nest here and wild goats that still roam. At its western tip, the large sand-spit beach is popular and has some facilities.

THE BASICS

☩ H4
✉ 14km (9 miles) south of Ólbia via Route 125
🍴 Ristorante da Tonino (▷ 61)
🚤 Infrequent service from Ólbia
🚢 Boats to the island from the kiosk at the beach in San Paolo (☎ 0789 40210)
♿ Few; terrain can be steep and rocky in places

HIGHLIGHTS

● View of the island from Porto San Paolo
● Beaches on Tavolara
● Hiking the island
● Beach at Porto San Paolo

Santa Teresa di Gallura

Looking down from the Aragonese tower (left); a winding path leads up to the tower (right)

THE BASICS

🚉 F1
✉ 60km (37 miles) northwest of Ólbia
🍴 Many restaurants and cafés
🚌 From Ólbia
⛴ Ferry to Corsica
♿ Few

HIGHLIGHTS

● The lively nightlife and bar scene
● Eroded rocks of Capo Testa
● Valle della Luna beach
● Sailing in the challenging winds of the Straits of Bonifacio

From the beach at Santa Teresa or the wild rocky headland of Capo Testa are sweeping views to the white cliffs of Corsica, 17km (10.5 miles) across the Straits of Bonifacio.

Defensive position Part of the Costa Smeralda geographically, and known for its buzzing nightlife, Santa Teresa has little else in common with its glitzy Johnny-come-lately neighbours. For one thing, it was there long before them, founded by King Emanuel I of Savoia as part of his defensive system to thwart Napoleon. Its orderly grid of streets centre on a wide square named for the king, and slope down to the small but very popular sand beach, Rena Bianca. From here a path leads up a headland to a round Aragonese tower, coastal defence from the days when Spain controlled the island.

Weird rocks Walkers can follow more trails through parkland over a high headland to reach Capo Testa, also accessible by road. These high rock promontories are so wildly eroded by wind that its formations seem otherworldly, so much so that one area has been named Valle della Luna (Valley of the Moon), not to be confused with the nearby mountain region of the same name. A small beach lies below its eerie white shapes, and more beaches hide in coves beneath others. A larger beach is at Báia de Santa Reparata, just out of Santa Teresa on the road to Capo Testa. Further beaches lie to the west, some with villages around them.

The town hall in Piazza Gallura (left); a street scene in Témpio Pausánia

Témpio Pausánia

The narrow streets through Témpio Pausánia's medieval heart are paved in granite stones set in a herringbone pattern between stone buildings that look as if they have grown there.

Granite and cork A mountain town constructed almost entirely of granite from nearby quarries, Témpio Pausánia built its fortunes on stone and cork. In fact, much of the cork in Italian wine bottles is from this mountain city.

Churches and *piazze* The substantial granite houses are softened by graceful wrought-iron balconies, and smart shops enliven the busy walking street of Via Roma, which leads from the city's spacious Piazza Gallura. A 17th-century Capuchin convent, now the town hall, forms one side of the square. The Cattedrale di San Pietro, built in the 12th-century and extended in the 15th, faces another smaller *piazza* along with two 16th-century oratorios. The former convent of St. Francis has a graceful cloister, while other notable churches are scattered about the city.

Stone fountains A long tree-lined promenade leads past Fonte Nuova, a stone fountain that descends in a series of pools. The therapeutic spa complex and a mineral spring is reached by a walk through the wooded park of San Lorenzo. Steam locomotives are displayed in the train museum, at the rail station, which is decorated with a frieze by artist Giuseppe Biasi.

THE BASICS

➕ F3
✉ 45km (28 miles) west of Ólbia
☎ 079 631 273
🍴 Many restaurants and cafés
🚍 From Ólbia
♿ Few

HIGHLIGHTS

● Medieval streets
● Climbing through San Lorenzo park to the atmospheric spa fountain
● The lively six-day Carnival, and its summer replay in August

DID YOU KNOW?

● The world's only institute to study the industrial potential of cork is located here.

More to See

ÁGGIUS

www.aggius.net

The particularly attractive mountain town of stone houses has a long history of carpet-weaving, which can be appreciated at the carpet exhibition staged all summer (▷ 60). This craft, along with several other traditional local trades—metalwork, cork and stone-cutting—as well as the needlework involved in local costumes, can be seen at the Museo Etnografico Olivia Carta Cannas (www.museomeoc.com), which also explores Sardinian traditions. The route through the dramatic Valle della Luna (▷ 57) begins in Ággius.

🚩 E3 ✉ Northwest of Témpio Pausánia 🍴 Restaurants and cafés 🚆 On the main line between Témpio Pausánia and Sássari ♿ Few

ARCIPÉLAGO DI LA MADDALENA BEACHES

www.lamaddalenapark.it

The islands of the archipelago have a number of good beaches but some may be out of bounds as part of the Parco Nazionale that encompasses all the islands. On La Maddalena use the Panoramico road that circles the island, looking for *spiaggia* signs. On Ísola Giardinelli, joined to La Maddalena on the east by a causeway, there are a few *cala* (coves) with beaches. On the main island look for Spiaggia Bassa Trinita, Spiaggia della Maddalena and Spiaggia Porto Massimo. Ísola Caprera is connected via a causeway and bridge; follow the road south at the fork towards Punto Rossa. There are beaches on the right of the road. On San Stefano a beach is opposite Isolotto Rosa. Beaches on uninhabited islands are accessible by boat tours from La Maddalena.

🚩 G2 ✉ Off Palau ☎ 0789 79021 🍴 Restaurants and cafés at La Maddalena 🚢 Saremar Ferry (☎ 0789 737 660; www.saremar.it); Demcomar Ferry (☎ 0789 739 088, 0781 857 123; www.delcomar.it). Tickets at the port, frequent departures ♿ None

The best beaches are on La Maddalena's north coast

BÁIA SARDINIA

Like much of the Costa Smeralda, this is a specially built resort town, but less precious than some. It overlooks a good white-sand beach surrounded by attractive Mediterranean architecture. A path along the shore leads past wind-sculpted rocks to a series of small beaches among dramatic outcrops of stone. The development of Poltu Quatu is a purpose-built village that is reminiscent of Greek island architecture.

➕ G2 ✉ Off SP59 west of Porto Cervo 🍽 Restaurants and cafés 🚌 Infrequent service from Porto Cervo ♿ Good

BÁIA SARDINIA: AQUADREAM WATER PARK

www.aquadream.it

The water park offers more water-splashing options than you would expect—there are slides, tubes, corkscrew tube tunnels, a river to float, pools, and more. You can have a hydromassage or even play mini-golf. Aquadream is associated with La Jacia Hotel and Resort.

➕ G2 ✉ Off SP59 at Báia Sardinia ☎ 0789 99511 🕐 Jun to mid-Sep daily 10–6 🍽 Café (€–€€) 🚌 Infrequent service from Porto Cervo ♿ Good 💶 Very expensive

CANNIGÍONE

Cannigíone is a lively little beach town, far more down-to-earth than neighbouring resorts just across the Gulf of Arzachena.

➕ G2 ✉ East of Arzachena 🍽 Plentiful 🚌 To Arzachena from Ólbia ♿ Few

GALLURA

Views to the south from the heights of Arzachena sweep across a foreground of rounded, eroded mountains to a horizon of steep, jagged peaks, while Gallura's coast is a succession of rocky promontories and idyllic beaches. Despite its more recent influx of coastal tourist development, a few kilometres inland is a mountainous wilderness broken only by granite towns and upland meadows full of grazing sheep. Few parts of Sardinia have

Báia Sardinia, a pristine, purpose-built resort

★

maintained such regional distinction as Gallura, where even the cuisine retains its own unique specialities, including the hearty and satisfying *zuppa Gallurese*.

➕ F3 ✉ Northwest of Ólbia
🍴 Restaurants and cafés in the towns
🚌 Service to major towns ♿ Few

GOLFO ARANCI

A busy ferry port connecting the Costa Smeralda to mainland Italy, Golfo Aranci is at the end of a long peninsula. An express road to the ferry terminal and rail station bypasses the town. Beyond the ferry terminal a road follows the shore to Cala Greco, and the beach at Cala Sabina, on the north shore of the peninsula, can be reached by train from the Golfo Aranci station. Look for beaches off the road to Ólbia, especially Spiaggia Rena Bianca, which has fine white sand and plentiful parking.

➕ H3 ✉ Northeast of Ólbia 🚌 To Ólbia and beyond 🍴 Plentiful ♿ Good
🚢 Connecting to Livorno and Civitavecchia

ÓLBIA

www.olbiaturismo.it

The importance of Ólbia to the traveller is its role as transportation hub. In summer its airport, Aeroporto Costa Smeralda, is one of the busiest in Europe. Its port is in constant movement with the arrival and departure of ferries from Genova, La Spezia, Livorno, Cittavecchia and Arbatax. The city itself has little to attract visitors, however Corso Umberto in the older part of the city is the place to go for the 11th-century Chiesa di San Simplicio, built of local granite, and for good restaurants. Inside are a variety of columns recycled from local Roman and earlier buildings. There are also 13th-century frescoes in the apse, one of which memorializes the martyrdom of the name saint, patron of the city. His feast day in mid-May makes the church the centrepiece of a three-day celebration.

➕ G3 ✉ Northeast coast, Costa Smeralda
☎ 0789 24696 🍴 Plentiful restaurants

Spiaggia Rena Bianca before the crowds arrive

Fishing boats moored in Ólbia's harbour

and cafés Regular service from Sássari and Cágliari From Ólbia airport to town centre Tirrenia (www.tirrenia.it); Moby Lines (www.mobylines.com); Sardinia Ferries (www.corsica-ferries.co.uk)

PORTO CERVO: MDM

www.mdmmuseum.it

This museum of modern art, opened in 2007, shows changing exhibits and offers cultural events and classes, some in co-operation with the Guggenheim in Venice. Its top-floor lounge-café has a terrace overlooking Porto Cervo, serving light food and champagnes.

🔢 H2 ✉ Via del Porto Vecchio 1 ☎ 0789 92225 🕐 Hours can vary 🍴 Café (€€) 🚌 From Ólbia 🚹 Good 💶 Inexpensive

SAN TEODORO

A small town that has grown into a resort area over the last few decades, San Teodoro is at the southern point of the Tavolara Marine Reserve. In the height of summer its famed white-sand beaches are crowded, but still pleasant. In addition to the beach in town, look for a number of others within a few kilometres. These include Spiaggia Insuledda, off the SP125 south of town at Ottiolu. and, on the Capo Coda Cavallo peninsula, Spiaggia dell'Impostu, and farther out Spiaggia Capo Coda Cavallo—both of these are off the SP125 north of town.

🔢 H4 ✉ SP125 south of Ólbia and Porto San Paolo 🍴 Restaurants and cafés 🚌 From Ólbia 🚹 Few

VALLE DELLA LUNA

After climbing steeply out of Àggius, a well-marked left turn leads immediately into a spectacular world of wildly eroded gigantic rock formations, convoluted granite shapes that loom overhead and protrude from the green pastures. The area is not large—the road through the valley is only 7km (4 miles) long, and the strange stone formations end as abruptly as they began.

🔢 E3 ✉ SP74 northwest of Témpio Pausánia

Rock formation in Valle della Luna (Moon Valley)

Témpio Pausánia

From medieval streets paved in granite blocks, climb through a green pine forest to an ancient mineral spring.

DISTANCE: 1.6km (1 mile)   **ALLOW:** 2 hours with stops

START

END

PIAZZA GALLURA
➕ F3

FONTE RINAGGIU
➕ F3

1 Begin in the wide Piazza Gallura, facing the town hall, the former convent of cloistered Capuchin nuns. Follow Via Roma, to the left, past the stone church, Chiesa Santa Croce.

7 At the top, follow Viale delle Fonti straight ahead through the formal gardens to the Fonte Rinaggiu, the mineral spring in a mossy hollow below. For sweeping views over the countryside, climb the steep hill behind the fountain.

2 Turn right into Piazza San Pietro to visit the cathedral, with its two fine carved altars and a medieval portal. Opposite is the little Oratorio del Rosario with a good baroque altar, and beside the cathedral is the Oratorio di Santa Croce.

6 Climb past the fountain to the tree-lined promenade above, turning right to follow the moss-covered steps and pathway through Pineta San Lorenzo, an open pine forest.

3 Return to Via Roma and continue past some smart shops to Piazza Italia, filled with cafés.

5 At the far end of the *largo*, follow Viale Fonte Nuova downhill alongside the park to the cascading Fonte Nuova.

4 Follow the stone-paved Via Gramisci between rows of granite buildings, taking the second right into the long Largo A. Gaspari. Turn left.

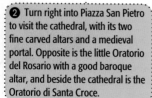

WALK

THE NORTHEAST

Shopping

AGGESE CARPET EXHIBITION
www.aggius.net
From early July through September, a carpet showroom is open, where visitors can see the finest examples of this local art.
🚏 E3 ✉ Aggius, near Témpio Pausánia
☎ 079 620 339

CASA MUNDULA
www.casamundula.com
At Casa Mundula you will find fine quality authentic crafts and foods, including handcrafted knives, filigree jewellery, embroidery, locally made pastas, honey, wine and preserved fruits.

🚏 F3 ✉ Via Roma 102, Témpio Pausánia
☎ 079 634 023

SARDINIAN CARPETS
Weaving carpets from the coarse fleece of Sardinian sheep has been an island industry for centuries, and although the wool is now coloured with chemical dyes instead of wild plants, weaving methods have changed very little. The traditional method produces a tight loop that stands above the surface, either in monochrome or contrasting colours, creating a thick, cushiony rug.

MDM MUSEUM BOOKSHOP
www.mdmmuseum.it
Art reproductions, art books and stylish contemporary wearable designs are sold at this shop in Porto Cervo's modern art museum.
🚏 H12 ✉ Via del Porto Vecchio 1, Porto Cervo
☎ 0789 92225

SARDEGNA IN FESTA
The outlet store of a maker of traditional *torrone*, a hazelnut and honey nougat made in Sardinia.
🚏 G2 ✉ Via Ogligastra Tonara, Loc. Tiana, Arzachena
☎ 0789 811 957

Entertainment and Activities

AREAMARE DIVING CENTER
www.areamare.com
Guided dives and lessons take place in the sheltered Gulf of Arzachena.
🚏 G2 ✉ Via Vespucci 52, Cannigione ☎ 338 822 1135

CAPRICORNO
A big and very popular disco, Capricorno has a smart contemporary ambience and never lacks action.
🚏 G3 ✉ Via Catello Piro 2, Ólbia ☎ 078 924 700
🕐 Daily 11pm–6am

CAVALLO MARSALLA CENTRO IPPICO
www.lamaddalena.it/barabo.htm
Guided horse trekking among the wild landscapes of Ísola Caprera.
🚏 G2 ✉ Località Stagnali, Ísola Caprera ☎ 347 235 9064 🕐 Open all year

CENTRO SERVIZI TURISTICI VERDEMARE
Diving, snorkelling and boat excursions to La Maddalena Archipelago and Costa Smeralda; also bike rentals.

🚏 G2 ✉ Via Nazionale 18, Cannigione ☎ 368 351 9386

DIVING CENTRE COSTA PARADISO
www.costaparadisodiving.it
Lessons and guided dives, taking advantage of the many beautiful dive sites off the north coast, where beginners can see brilliant Mediterranean sea life.
🚏 F1 ✉ Li Cossi beach, Costa Paradiso, 35km (22 miles) from Santa Teresa di Gallura ☎ 079 688 027
🕐 Summer, dives at 8.30am, 10.30am, 2.30pm and 4pm

MOTONAVE *LADY LUNA*

www.giteinbarca.it
This fun, all-day cruise aboard the *Lady Luna* traverses the Parco Nazionale dell'Arcipélago di La Maddalena, taking in all of the major islands and stopping for swimming along the way. Lunch is provided. Reservations by phone are encouraged.
🚩 G2 ✉ Landing 7 at the dock in front of the Stazione Marittima, Palau ☎ 339 387 7196, 328 658 2193 🕐 Daily departures 10.45, return 5.30

PRO CENTER MICHIEL BOUWMEESTER

www.procenter.it/WINDSURF
Windsurfing rentals and a school taking full advantage of the steady winds off the north coast. The professional instructors follow a graded teaching scheme.
🚩 G2 ✉ The Windsurf Village, Baia Delfino, Loc. Porto Pollo, Palau ☎ 0789 704 206, 335 637 9949 🕐 Apr–Oct

SOPRAVENTO

DJs and live acts perform here, even in the winter, when the rest of the town is almost dead.
🚩 H2 ✉ Via Golfo Pevero, Porto Cervo ☎ 366 523 9322

Restaurants

CAFFÈ DEL MARE (€)

Bright, friendly spot for a sandwich, pasta, light meal or drink, in the centre of town.
🚩 F1 ✉ Pzza San Vittorio 14, Santa Teresa di Gallura ☎ 393 736 8936 🕐 Daily lunch and dinner

DA NARDINO RISTORANTE PIZZERIA (€€)

www.nardino.com
Pizza is available in the evening only, but the full menu has plenty of choices, with a strong emphasis on impeccably fresh seafood. It's one of the few places where the bread basket is filled with *pane gittau*—the local crisp flat bread split and re-baked with olive oil and salt.
🚩 H4 ✉ Via San Francesco 4, San Teodoro ☎ 0784 865 235 🕐 Thu–Tue 12.30–3, 7–12

FIT FOR A KING

Owned and presided over by the king of Tavolara, Tonino Bertoleoni, Ristorante da Tonino (€€) is more than a curiosity. Fresh seafood is carefully prepared and served on a terrace overlooking the beach. No credit cards are accepted.
🚩 H4 ✉ Via Tavolara 18, Ísola Tavolara ☎ 0789 58 570 🕐 Lunch and dinner Wed–Mon; summer only 🚤 Regular service from Porto San Paulo

ENOTECA DA LIÒ (€–€€)

Savour wines from Sardinian vineyards and farther afield at this friendly local spot, a favourite of those who step off their boats in the little harbour down the street. The menu features traditional local dishes.
🚩 G2 ✉ Corso Vittorio Emanuele 6, La Maddalena ☎ 0789 737 507 🕐 Meals served Tue–Sun 12–2, 8–10 🚤 Close to ferry from Palau

ISAEBI (€€–€€€)

www.isaebi.it
Those who have a

hankering for something other than Sardinian dishes will find sushi, sashimi and Asian fusion dishes in the serene setting of this restaurant in a historic house right on the harbour.

✚ G2 ✉ Via S. Stefano 12–15, La Maddalena ☎ 078 973 7326 🕙 Dinner Tue–Sun 🚢 Directly opposite ferry from Palau

IL MAESTRALE (€€)

The menu at this restaurant, grill and pizzeria offers a good variety. *Porchetto al mirto* (roast suckling pig served on a fragrant bed of myrtle) cooked in a wood-fired oven is a speciality by reservation.

✚ G2 ✉ Località Malchittu, Arzachena (in front of the Nuraghe Albucciu) ☎ 0789 81571 🕙 Daily lunch and dinner

NORTH WEST RISTORANTE (€€)

The only hint of the surprisingly elegant little dining room hidden behind a café/bar is the blackboard on the street announcing the day's special, which might be roast suckling pig or the delicious *zuppa Gallurese*. The bar serves far better sandwiches than most. No credit cards are accepted.

✚ F3 ✉ Via Calagianis 13, San Antonio di Gallura ☎ 079 669 403, 079 669 144 🕙 Daily 12.30–3, 7.30–10; closed Mon winter

RISTORANTE BAR MUSEUM (€€)

Walk through the attractive café (with tasty baked goods) to find the restaurant, where daily specials supplement a menu of traditional Galluran dishes. The café spills into the town's main *piazza*, which is an excellent vantage point for watching local life over an *aperitivo*.

✚ F3 ✉ Piazza Gallura 27, Témpio Pausánia ☎ 079 671 083 🕙 Daily lunch and dinner

TENUTA PILASTRU (€€)

www.tenutapilastru.it
One of the island's best restaurants, set in a beautiful *agriturismo* high in the hills, features either an à la carte menu or a fixed full meal of Sardinian specialities. This multi-course feast begins

ZUPPA GALLURESE

While restaurants in Gallura serve many of the Sardinian favourites, they have a few unique to the region. Most notable is *zuppa Gallurese*, which is not a soup, but a baked dish made of the simplest of ingredients: dried slices of bread, local sheep cheese and broth. Much of the rich flavour is determined by the latter, which might be lamb or beef, and seasoned with fragrant herbs from the *macchia*.

with plates of smoked ricotta, local salami, stuffed roasted peppers and more, followed by hand-made *culurgiones* (▷ 14) and *zuppa Gallurese* (▷ panel). The main course includes roast suckling pig and braised lamb.

✚ G2 ✉ loc. Pilastru, Arzachena ☎ 0789 82936 🕙 Mon–Sat dinner, Sun lunch

TRATTORIA LA GALLURESE (€–€€)

The atmospheric upstairs dining room is hidden above a tiny entry. The family-operated trattoria makes delectable filled pastas in-house, including a particularly tasty *ravioli dolci* made with lemon. Their *zuppa Gallurese* is one of the best.

✚ F3 ✉ Via Novara 2, Témpio Pausánia ☎ 079 6393012 🕙 Daily 12–3.30, 7–10.15

IL VECCHIO MULINO (€€)

www.ilvecchiomulinoristorante. com
This popular local restaurant offers the dual specialities of grilled and roasted Sardinian-raised meats and pizza baked in a wood oven. The servings are bountiful and the steaks are some of the best around.

✚ G2 ✉ SS125 Località Moro, Arzachena ☎ 0789 81943 🕙 Daily lunch and dinner

Sardinia's west coast is punctuated by major historic sites that form a timeline of island history: a major Nuraghe and sacred well, a Phoenician and later Roman port city, and the elegant capital city of one of Sardinia's four medieval kingdoms. Birders flock to the lagoons where rare birds nest.

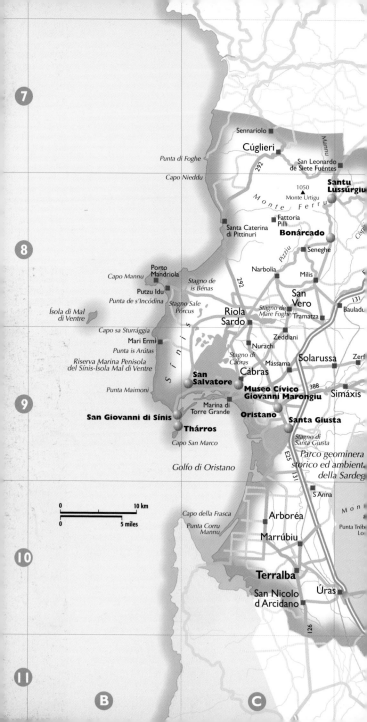

Sennariolo

Cúglieri

Punta di Foghe

San Leonardo
de Siete Fuéntes

Capo Nieddu

**Santu
Lussúrgiu**

1050
Monte Urtigu
Monte Ferru

Fattoria
Pilli

Santa Caterina
di Pittinuri

Bonárcado

Seneghe

Porto
Mandriola

Capo Mannu

Narbolia

Milis

Stagno de
is Bénas

**San
Vero**

Putzu Idu

Punta de s'Incódina

131

Stagno Sale
Pórcus

**Riola
Sardo**

Stagno de
Mare Foghe

Tramatza

Bauladu

Ísola di Mal
di Ventre

Capo sa Sturrággia

Mari Ermi

Zeddiani

Nurachi

Solarussa

Zerf

Punta is Arútas

S í n i s

Stagno di
Cábras

Mássama

Riserva Marina Penísola
del Sínis-Ísola Mal di Ventre

Cábras

Punta Maimoni

**San
Salvatore**

**Museo Cívico
Giovanni Marongiu**

388

Simáxis

San Giovanni di Sínis

Marina di
Torre Grande

Oristano

Thárros

Santa Giusta

Capo San Marco

Stagno di
Santa Giusta

Golfo di Oristano

E25
131

*Parco geominera
storico ed ambient.
della Sardeg*

S Anna

0   10 km
0   5 miles

Capo della Frasca

Arboréa

Mon

Punta Corru
Mannu

Marrúbiu

Punta Tréb
Lo

Terralba

Úras

San Nicolo
d'Arcidano

126

Mannu

292

Cisp

Pizziu

B

C

7

8

9

10

11

Nuraghe Losa

HIGHLIGHTS

● The large, harmonious central chamber
● Stone-paved spiral passageways hidden inside the walls

TIP

● To better appreciate the stonework inside the passageways, carry a torch.

Rare for Nuraghi, Losa is illuminated inside by recessed lamps, so visitors can admire the genius of its stone *thalos* domes and navigate its maze of fascinating interior passageways.

Stone bastion One of the three most important Nuraghi in Sardinia, Losa is the most complex, its inside tower surrounded by three smaller towers that form a single tri-lobed bastion with a stone passageway spiralling up inside its massive thick walls to the upper floors. The second floor remains intact, with its roof complete. As in other Nuraghi, each level is roofed with a *thalos* method, instead of a true dome. In these, each succeeding course of stone overhangs inward from the last until they meet at the top.

Remains of the cone tower in the shape of a beehive (far left, top right and bottom right); neocropolis detail (top middle); the illuminated inside chamber (bottom middle)

A thousand years of use Part of a later defensive wall remains outside, with the remains of two towers. The central room of the main tower is one of the largest, and its refined construction is in excellent condition. It dates from the end of the Middle Bronze Age—about the 12th to 14th century BC. Finds uncovered here show the site was largely in continuous use for more than 1,000 years, through the Punic era (fourth century BC), through Roman times and into the Byzantine era of the seventh and eighth centuries AD. Unlike many of other Nuraghi, the surrounding village has not been excavated.

Admire the artefacts A little one-room museum at the site displays artefacts found there and elsewhere, including bronze bracelets with geometric decoration.

THE BASICS

www.nuraghelosa.net
+ D8
✉ Off SS131 at Abasanta
☎ 0785 52302
🕐 Daily winter 9–5; summer 9–7
🍴 Café at entrance; closed winter (€)
🚌 From Oristano to Abasanta, then 3km (2-mile) walk
♿ Few
💶 Moderate
❓ The small shop has a good selection of reference books

THE WEST ★ TOP 25

67

Oristano

TOP 25

THE WEST

TOP 25

HIGHLIGHTS

- Antiquarium Arborense
- Torre di San Cristoforo
- Duomo of Santa Maria
- Thárros (▷ 71)

TIP

- Be there in early February for the Festival of Sa Sartiglia, an extravaganza of spirited horse riding, medieval pageantry and costumes.

In the 11th century, people from Thárros fled the coast to escape pirates and other attackers, and founded Oristano. Once the capital of the kingdom of Arborea, it is now a centre of ceramic manufacture.

Medieval capital Wandering the narrow winding streets of the small, well-preserved city, it is easy to imagine life here in medieval times. In 1070 the Giudicatta of Arborea, one of the four medieval kingdoms on the island, adopted it as its capital. Torre di San Cristoforo, a tall two-tiered tower in Piazza Roma, was once part of the town walls, built in 1291 by order of King Mariano II. The Duomo of Santa Maria, also built during his reign (1288), was greatly changed by renovation in the 18th and 19th centuries. Its colourful tiled domes

Clockwise from far left: Campanile of the Duomo of Santa Maria; Torre de San Cristoforo tower; San Francesco church; statue of Queen Eleonora in Piazza Eleonora d'Arborea

reflect the Aragonese influence at the time of its renovation. Eleanora of Arborea, the most famed of Sardinian monarchs (1383–1404) and a remarkable leader still admired today (Sardinians call her their Joan of Arc), gave the island its first codified laws.

Other attractions At the south end of the Via Umberto in Piazza Eleanora, the town hall occupies a former monastery, and the church of the Assumption is an amalgam of styles centring on the baroque. Opposite is the neoclassical church of San Francesco, which contains the Nicodemo crucifix, a fine example of Spanish Gothic sculpture from the Aragonese period. Treasures recovered from the nearby archeological ruins of Thárros are preserved in the city's Antiquarium Arborense museum.

THE BASICS

🗺 C9
✉ Midway along the west coast on route SS131
🍴 Numerous
🚆 From Cágliari
🚌 From Cágliari and Sássari
♿ Few

Santa Cristina

TOP 25

A stone dwelling, once home to monks (left); the entrance to the sacred temple (right)

THE BASICS

🔳 D8

✉ SS131, Località Santa Cristina, Paulilatino

☎ 0785 55438

🕐 Apr–Aug daily 8.30am–11pm; Sep–Mar 8.30am–9pm

🍴 Café at entrance (€)

♿ Holy well: good

💰 Moderate; includes admission to Palazzo Atzori Museum in Paulilatino

❓ Shop with reference books and local crafts

HIGHLIGHTS

● Rectangular hut with *thalos* roof

● A Nuraghe with a wild garden on top

● Spring and autumn equinoxes, when the morning sun lights the stairs, reaching the water in the sacred well

This three-for-one site includes a small Nuraghic village, a sacred well and a later Christian pilgrim village and church, still the scene of an annual pilgrimage.

Holy well The well temple, which dates from 1200–1100BC, is set inside a circular wall, and consists of a wide stairway of smoothly worked stones leading down to a conical chamber with a *thalos* dome (made of concentric rings of stone that leave a smaller opening with each course). The last course of stones in the roof, instead of covering it completely, forms an open skylight at ground level. In wet seasons the spring fills the floor of the chamber to the level of the bottom step.

Wildflowers on top Now surrounded by trees, Santa Cristina is very atmospheric, its stone village green with moss and grass and the tower itself crowned with wildflowers. A torch is essential to see the interior, and a climb to the open roof is rewarded with a fine view. It is a single tower built of irregular basalt. Two of the huts in the surrounding village are long and narrow, instead of round, and the stone roof of one is intact.

Pilgrim village Between the well and the Nuraghe is a church founded in the 12th century. Around it are rows of tiny attached stone dwellings that were once home to monks, and now houses those who make the pilgrimages here in May and October.

The blue sea provides a perfect backdrop for the site (left); Torre Spagnola (right)

Nuraghic, Phoenician, Punic and Roman cultures met, mingled and melted away on this rocky point of land located on the Sínis Peninsula.

Phoenicians Around 800BC the Phoenicians came to trade for copper and lead with the Stone Age Nuraghic settlement on the ridge, and established a community. Their *tophet*—burial ground for children—is among the remains of the Nuraghic village. Phoenicians stayed until about 650BC, when Carthaginian warriors took over, followed by Roman legions in the Punic Wars in 238BC. Thárros continued to grow and prosper long into Roman times.

Its stones built Oristano The stones of abandoned Thárros were taken away by the cartload to build Oristano after 550BC. What remains today are the lower walls and foundations, tracing the city's floor-plan across the sloping point.

Picturing Thárros as it was Roman streets radiate from the broad granite-paved Cardo Maximus, the main street, and remains of the Roman aqueduct, two baths, temples, a baptistry, shops and homes line them, many with their doorsteps still intact. A Roman amphitheatre overlooks the sea, and Carthaginian defensive walls and a moat still separate the city's inland side from the rest of the peninsula. Later, the Spanish built a tall stone tower on a hilltop above the ruins.

THE BASICS

⊞ B9
✉ Cábras, 20km (12 miles) west of Oristano
☎ 0783 397 306
🕐 Apr–Oct daily 9–1, 4–8; Nov–Mar 10–1, 3–7
🍴 Bar at entrance (€); trattoria nearby (€–€€)
🚌 From Oristano in summer only
♿ None
💰 Moderate, includes Museo Cívico Giovanni Marongiu, Cábras (▷ 72)

HIGHLIGHTS

● Phoenician *tophet* on Su Muru Mannu hill
● Terme di Convento Vecchio
● Walking the Roman streets
● Amphitheatre
● Carthaginian walls and moat

More to See

BONÁRCADO
The small stone town, known for its olive oil, climbs the slopes of Monte Ferru, surrounded by cork forests, olive and orange groves. Below, the Romanesque Chiesa di Santa Maria, a small Byzantine sanctuary built over the remains of a Roman bath, retains one pool intact, and a venerated 15th-century bas-relief of the Virgin Mary.

🖶 C8 ✉ 25km (15.5 miles) north of Oristano 🍴 Few 🚌 Infrequent service from Paulilatino 🚹 None

FORDONGIÁNUS
Prosperous even in Roman times, Fordongiánus has the extensive remains of Roman baths, built at thermal springs from which hot mineral-laden water still flows. The town is renowned for the distinctive local red trachyte stone. On the SS388, towards Oristano, stands the small monastery of San Lussorio, built about 1100 on an older structure.

🖶 D9 ✉ SS388 northeast of Ólbia

🕐 Thermal spring always open; baths visible when gate is closed 🍴 A few 🚌 From Cágliari and Oristano 🚹 None 🖐 Inexpensive

MUSEO CÍVICO GIOVANNI MARONGIU
Carved stone stele, funerary urns and smaller finds from the Thárros Phoenician *tophet* are displayed here, positioned as originally found. Other collections explore the local reed fishing boats, a Roman shipwreck that was found nearby, neolithic flint and obsidian tools and Roman glasswork.

🖶 C9 ✉ Via Thárros 121, Cábras ☎ 0783 290 636 🕐 Apr–Oct daily 9–1, 4–8; Nov–Mar 10–1, 3–7 🍴 Nearby 🚹 Good 🖐 Moderate (included in Thárros admission ▷ 71)

SAN GIOVANNI DI SÍNIS
www.areamarinasinis.it
The small 6th-century Byzantine church of San Giovanni di Sínis, one of the oldest in Sardinia, has barrel vaults, a cupola ceiling and a

Ruins of the ancient Roman spa in Fordongiánus

baptismal font with a fish carved on it. At the beach is the visitor centre of the Marine Protected Area, which shows videos about the marine environment.

✚ B9 ✉ San Giovanni di Sínis ☎ 0783 371 006 🍴 Nearby 🚌 From Oristano in summer only ♿ Good 🎟 Free

SAN SALVATORE

Close to the Thárros road, this dusty little village is home to the Sanctuary of San Salvatore, around which are *cumbessias*, small one-floor houses. These houses are used by pilgrims during the saint's August festival, when the village comes alive. Fans of 'spaghetti westerns' may recognize this town as a setting.

✚ C9 ✉ West of Oristano 🍴 Few ♿ None

SANTA GIUSTA

Santa Giusta's fine 12th-century cathedral, its tower rising high above the town, is remarkable for its re-use of Roman capitals and columns in the nave and crypt; no two are alike, varying in shape, decoration, even type of stone. The first chapel on the right (light switch left) has frescoed walls and ceiling and a gilded polychrome altarpiece. In a crypt under the main altar (light switch right), the relics of Santa Giusta are kept in a glass chest. At San Severn church is a Phoenician necropolis.

✚ C9 ✉ 3km (2 miles) south of Oristano 🍴 A few 🚌 From Oristano ♿ None

SANTU LUSSÚRGIU

www.comunesantulussurgiu.it

Nestled in the crater of the ancient volcano of Monte Ferru, Santu Lussúrgiu is approached from high above, the road descending into town. Through the stone arch next to the 19th-century Chiesa San Pietro, narrow streets of stone houses wind and climb through the old medieval town. Look for wall murals of horses, and for fine hand-made knives (▷ 75).

✚ C8 ✉ North of Oristano 🍴 Several 🚌 From Bonárcado and Oristano ♿ None

The medieval town of Santa Lussúrgiu

Houses in San Salvatore

The Sínis Peninsula

From beaches and lagoons filled with birds during migration seasons to a sixth-century church and a city founded by Phoenicians.

DISTANCE: 53km (33 miles) **ALLOW:** half a day with stops

START

ORISTANO
✚ C9

1 Leave Oristano heading north on the SS292 towards Torre Grande, turning left at signs to Cábras and Thárros, for a stop at the busy beach resort town of Marina Torre Grande.

2 Return to the main road, turning left, signposted to San Giovanni di Sínis. The road lies between lagoons filled with flamingos, and walking paths lead to closer looks at the birdlife, especially abundant during spring and fall migrations.

3 Bear left to San Giovanni di Sínis, where the sixth-century church, one of the oldest in Sardinia, stands opposite the visitors' centre for the Sínis Peninsula Marine Reserve.

4 Continue on to Thárros (▷ 71), founded as a trading port by Phoenicians in the ninth century BC on an older Nuraghic site.

END

ORISTANO
✚ C9

7 Return to the main road, bearing right to Riolo Sardo, where another right turn onto the SS292 leads back to Oristano.

6 Continue north, making a side-track left to the beach, Spiaggiadi Is Arutas, past the Nuraghe Piscina Rubia.

5 Backtrack to the left turn marked San Salvatore (▷ 73), following it to that strange little village of one-storey summer homes, frequently used as a stage set for 'spaghetti western' films.

Shopping

CANTINA SOCIALE DELLE VERNACCIA DI ORISTANO

www.vinovernaccia.com
Local winery and distillery producing red, white, rosé and a *grappa di vernaccia*, all from traditional Sardinian vines.
🔢 C8 ✉ Via Oristano 6A, Oristano ☎ 0783 33155

DISTILLERIE LUSSURGESI

www.abbardente.it
Local distillers of fine *acquavitae*, grappa and brandy. They are also chocolate makers.

🔢 C8 ✉ Via delle Sorgente 8, Santu Lussúrgiu ☎ 0783 552 037

ORISTANO MARKET

Where the local people and restaurant chefs come to buy their locally produced foods.
🔢 C9 ✉ Via Costa and Via Mazzini, Oristano 🕐 Mon–Sat morning

SALARIS BROTHERS

www.salariscoltelli.it
Descended from a long line of blacksmiths, the company specializes in fine handmade knives

in Damascus steel with horn or rare wood handles. They also produce fine bits for horses, including custom-made pieces. Fine knives are one of the primary handicrafts of the island.
🔢 C8 ✉ Viale Azuni 183, Santu Lussúrgiu ☎ 0783 550 287

SPECIALITA SARDE

Gourmet food shop selling Sardinian specialities; get your *bottarga* (Sicilian caviar) here.
🔢 C9 ✉ Via Figoli 41, Oristano ☎ 0783 72725

Entertainment and Activities

CLUB IS ARENAS

www.golfhotelisarenas.com
Set in a pine forest, the 18-hole par 72 golf course is close to the beach; the mild climate permits play year-round.
🔢 C8 ✉ Pineta Is Arenas, SS292, Narbolia ☎ 0783 529 011

DISCO KILL TIME

Don't expect citified nightlife in Oristano, but this popular disco is in the suburb of Santa Giusta.
🔢 C9 ✉ Via Garibaldi, Santa Giusta ☎ 0783 358 038

OLTREMARE

www.oltremare.sardegna.it
Guided diving at spots near Thárros. Also

SA SARTIGLIA

February brings carnival celebrations all over the island, but none is as spectacular as Oristano's *Sa Sartiglia*. Part equestrian tournament of medieval origins, part street party, its highlight is when masked riders, standing up in their saddles while their horses race at top speed, attempt to run their swords through a small metal star suspended over the street. Drums roll, trumpets flourish and the crowd cheers as each skilled horseman races past. Later the masked riders perform acrobatic tricks on horseback.

snorkelling trips, surfing and wind and kite surfing.
🔢 B9 ✉ San Giovanni di Sínis ☎ 346 758 9348

TEATRO GARAU

Theatre, dance and music, from musical comedy to classical choral and orchestral concerts.
🔢 C9 ✉ Via Parpaglia, Oristano ☎ 0783 78886

VISITOR CENTRE OF MARINE PROTECTED AREA

www.areamarinasinis.it
Fishing excursions using historic-style boats, and other environmental programmes.
🔢 B9 ✉ San Giovanni di Sínis ☎ 0783 371 006

Restaurants

AL BUE ROSSO (€€–€€€)

The *osteria* has only about a dozen tables in a converted century-old cheese dairy, where an experienced chef does creative takes with the outstanding local 'red ox' beef.

➕ C8 ✉ Piazzale Montiferru 3, Seneghe ☎ 0783 54384 🕐 Tue–Sun lunch and dinner; Nov–Mar closed dinner Tue and Wed

ANTICA DIMORA DEL GRUCCIONE (€–€€)

www.anticadimora.com
The focus here is on local produce, provisions, wines, cheeses and Sardinian products. The restaurant is an award-winning member of the Slow Food movement. Try *cestini di casizolu con fregola al sugo di capretto*, a Sardinian pasta and kid dish served with *casizolu* cheese.

➕ C8 ✉ Via Michelle Obino 31, Santu Lussúrgiu ☎ 0783 552 035 🕐 Daily dinner

LA BOCCA DEL VULCANO (€€–€€€)

At this family-run restaurant the chef does wondrous things with wild boar—perhaps paired with earthy local ceps, in a *ragu* sauce with ravioli or cured as *prosciutto di cinghiale*. Savour these on the outdoor terrace in good weather.

➕ C8 ✉ Via Alagon 27, Santu Lussúrgiu ☎ 0783 550 974 🕐 Lunch daily, dinner Mon–Sat

CRAF (€€)

In this former granary, you can dine under stone vaulting from the 1600s, on seasonal specialities like roast kid with artichokes or on fresh-caught local seafood.

➕ C9 ✉ Via De Castro 34, Oristano ☎ 0783 70666 🕐 Mon–Sat lunch and dinner

IL NAVIGLIO (€–€€)

While the menu leans towards the standard

BOTTARGA

The delicate flavour of Sardinian mullet roe (Sardinian caviar) has been appreciated in Italy for centuries, and the very best comes from the quiet waters of Stagno di Cábras, the large lagoon north of Oristano. Egg sacs are carefully removed, salted and laid out to air-dry almost as the mullet leaves the water. It is found in restaurants, stirred into piping hot dishes of pasta, or you can buy it at markets and gourmet shops, either whole or powdered.

Sardinian items, these are well prepared and flavourful, bringing locals to this location overlooking the town. Parking can be problematic.

➕ D9 ✉ Via Ipsitani 11–13, Fordongiánus ☎ 0783 60313 🕐 Daily lunch and dinner

RESTAURANT COCCO & DESSÌ (€€€)

www.ristorantecoccodessi.com
Behind a grand facade, this smart little place offers a unique dining experience in a land where menu variation is slim. Expect dishes such as *calamari* with citrus fruits or tagliatelle pasta with mussels and courgette (zucchini) blossoms. There's also an outstanding cheese selection.

➕ C8 ✉ Via Tirso 31, Oristano ☎ 0783 300 720 🕐 Tue–Sun lunch, Tue–Sat dinner; closed Jan

SA FUNTA (€€–€€€)

The setting overlooking the lagoon suggests the nautical decor, so it's not surprising to find seafood their speciality. Traditional recipes are updated a bit; especially delicious is the *seppiette alla vernaccia*, baby *calamari* prepared with the local amber wine.

➕ C8 ✉ Via Garibaldi 25, Cábras ☎ 0783 290 685 🕐 Mon–Sat 1–2.45, 8.15–10.30 🚌 From Oristano ❓ No credit cards

The real wonder of Sardinia's coast is not the rapid development of its tourist complexes in the past few decades, but that so much of it is still wildly beautiful. Nowhere is this better appreciated than around the Gulf of Orosei, behind which rise the rugged crags of Sardinia's highest mountains.

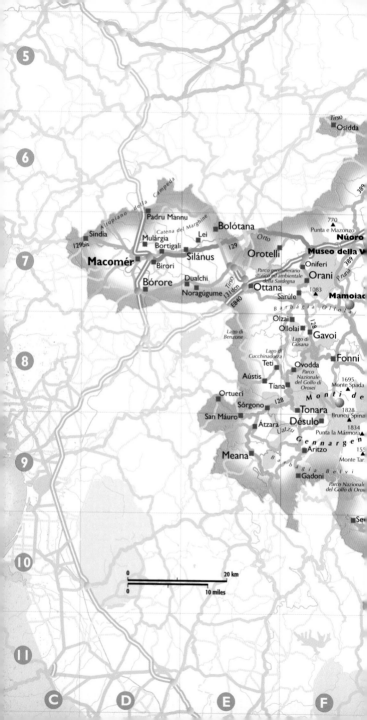

Brunella
Talavà
Cóncas
Torpè
Posada
Punta Orvili
la Caletta
Àfana
1019
Punta sa Donna
S S Annunziata
Sant'
Anna
Lodè
Santa Lucia
Mamone
Siniscóla
125
Parco geominerario
storico ed ambientale
della Sardegna
Capo Comino
Capo
Comino
99
Bitti
Onani
Bérchidda
Norghio
Lula
Sos
Álinos
Orune
Monte Creia
Punta Ginepro
Cala Fuile e Mare
Isalle
Irgoli
Galtelli
Onifai
125
S'Ena e Thomes
Orosei
Punta Nera
955
Monte
Ortobene
129
Serra Orrios
Lago del
Cedrino
Ofiena
Dorgali
Oliena
Cala Gonone
1463
Monte Corrasi
Tiscali
Golfo di Orosei
rgosolo
1416
Punta sa
Pruna
Parco Nazionale
del Golfo di Orosei
Cala di Luna
Gola Su
Gorroppu
Cala Sisine
1316
Monte Novo
an Giovanni
Punta Madaloro
Punta dell' Àcqua
Punta Caroddi
Urzulei
Capo di
Monte Santu
125
811
Talána
Triei
Punta Ginnircu
Baunei
Punta
Pedra Longa
Santa Maria
Navarrese
Villanova
Strisáili
Lotzorai
Girasole
Villagrande
Árzana
Tortolí
Àrbatax
Capo Bellavista
Lago alto
Flumendosa
1236
Monte Orru
Ilbono
Tortoli
Punta Nera
Gáiro
quisara
Lanusei
Gáiro
Bari
Punta su Mástixi
Jssássai
Ulássai
Jerzu
Cardedu
1008
Punta Coróngiu
o del
mineddu
Tertenía
876
Monte Ferru
Capo Sferracavallo
Perdasdefogu
Punta Moros
Melisenda
Porto Santoru
Capo Palmeri
Punta de sa Cala

Golfo di Orosei

TOP
25

HIGHLIGHTS

- Grotta del Bue Marino
- Small cove beaches
- Boating in the Gulf
- Wilderness of the Parco Nazionale de Golfo di Orosei

TIP

- The crystal-clear waters surrounding the coves provide wonderful snorkelling opportunities.

A rare sight, this coast is an untouched natural paradise with hidden beaches, a beautiful natural grotto and rugged rocky cliffs between the turquoise water and the green *macchia* and oak forests.

Natural shoreline Much of the coast of the Gulf of Orosei is protected as part of the Parco Nazionale de Golfo di Orosei, which also includes the eastern slopes of the Sopramonte. From the village of Cala Gonone in the north to Santa Maria Navarese in the south, there are no towns, and only one road runs along the entire shoreline.

Walk to beaches Cala Gonone is the starting point for exploring this spectacular coast. Sitting on a gentle hillside that leads down to the sea

The spectacular setting of Cala Gonone (left); clear as mineral water, the sea at Marina di Orosei beach (right)

edge, it started life as a fishing village but has prospered with the advent of tourism. The town itself has nice beaches opposite the port, which are accessible by foot. The more remote Cala Fuili beach is also accessible on foot via a path from the short coast road. It is possible to reach the Grotto del Bue Marino on foot, but it is best accessed by boat.

Sea caves The Grotta del Bue Marino takes its name from the monk seals that once inhabited the area, but which have not been seen recently. The grotto is a stunningly beautiful cave. Along the coast north of Cala Gonone is the Grotta di Ispinigoli, with a 38m (125ft) stalagmite. Access to the caves and secluded beaches is available by boat or by renting kayaks and canoes in Cala Gonone.

THE BASICS

✚ H7
✉ Off the coastal highway south of Dorgali
🍽 A few beach kiosks
🚌 Shuttle from Dorgali
🚢 Boats and kayak/canoe to beaches and grottos at the waterfront
♿ Few
💶 Boat trips expensive

Monti del Gennargentu

TOP 25

Goats are a common sight on the mountainside (left); wild flora (right)

THE BASICS

🔲 F8
✉ South of Núoro
🍴 Ristorante Barbagia (Via Umberto 6, Fonni; 078 058 4329; €€)
🚌 Infrequent service between Núoro and mountain towns
♿ None

HIGHLIGHTS

● High stone-capped mountains
● Museo delle Maschere Mediterranee at Mamoiada (▷ 85)
● Isolated shepherd huts
● Vineyards and sheep

TIP

● Take the Green Train from Mandas, skirting and climbing through the Gennargentu range to the east coast at Arbatax.

Wild and beautiful, the Monti del Gennargentu are the tallest of all the island's mountains, topping off at 1,834m (6,017ft). Snowcapped in winter, this is a rugged refuge for hardy people.

Land of Barbarians The mountains of Gennargentu were so inhospitable that dissidents escaped Roman rulers to these wild mountains and were never suppressed. This unruly lot earned the Roman epithet of Barbarians, root of the region's name, Barbagia. During the 18th and 19th centuries the oak forests that covered the mountains were cut for charcoal used in smelting ore, leaving only barren peaks. Mule trails from that time provide hiking trails today, and remnants of the charcoal-makers' trade can still be found.

See mainland Italy From the road between Fonni and Desulo, a narrow mountain road leads towards the summit of 1,829m (6,000ft) Bruncu Spina, the island's second-highest peak with its only ski area. Its one lift and two trails do not make it an international ski destination. From there a trail leads south over the Punta Paulinu to the tallest peak, Punta La Mármora (1,834m/6,016ft), with views across most of the island and even to the Italian mainland.

Sheep-herders' villages Among the joys of the Genargentu are the small villages perched high on mountain slopes, where many still earn their livelihood as herdsmen.

Hiking down from Mount Tiscali (left); a Nuraghic village (right)

Tiscali

One of the great mysteries of the Nuraghic period, here prehistoric people built their community, hidden inside a collapsed mountain cave high in the top of the Sopramonte mountain range.

Still a mystery Ever since archaeologists first examined it in the 1930s, the Nuraghic site at the top of 515m (1,690ft) Mount Tiscali has not disclosed its age. Most probably it was built in the late Nuraghic period, perhaps when locals were under pressure from invading Romans.

Cave village The remote village is contained in the walls of the collapsed cave, with some parts within the cave's tunnels. Near the entrance, the remains of 40 buildings form the main part of the settlement. Near by are remains of another group of about 20 smaller rectangular structures, probably for animals or storage. Unlike most other Nuraghic sites, it had no defensive tower.

Remote and rugged The site's inhospitality underlines the mystery surrounding it. Essentially without a water supply and lacking fertile land, existence must have been tenuous at best. Because of the terrain and unclear trails, it is important to visit with a guide from the Cooperativo Ghivine, an organization dedicated to preservation of the history and environment of the Sopramonte. Tours, taking an entire day, require a four-wheel-drive vehicle and mountain hikes of about 90 minutes each way.

THE BASICS

www.ghivine.com/
excursions.htm
🚩 G7
✉ Coop. Ghivine, Via Lamaramora 69e, Dorgali
☎ 0784 96721 or 338 834 1618
🕐 Nov–Apr 9–5; May–Oct 9–7; tours by reservation
♿ None
💷 Moderate

HIGHLIGHTS

● Unique Nuraghic ruins
● Mountain views
● Hiking excursion in the mountains

TIP

● Cooperativo Ghivine conducts excursions to other sites in the region including hikes in gorges and to hidden beaches on the Gulf of Orosei.

DEIPARAE VIRGINI A NIVE SACRUM

More to See

DORGALI

A small market town high in the mountains, Dorgali is a good place to shop for handicrafts, especially in leather, wool, cork and silver. The Grotta di Ispinigoli, with the longest stalagmite in Europe (38m/125ft), is open to the public.

➕ G7 ✉ South of Orosei on SS125
🍴 Numerous 🚌 Infrequent service from Orosei ♿ Few

DORGALI: SERRA ORRIOS

www.ilportalesardo.it

One of the island's best-preserved Nuraghic villages, Serra Orrios dates from the mid- and late Bronze Age and contains walls of about 100 houses and two religious structures in superb condition. Excavated finds are in Dorgali's Archaeological Museum on Via Mármora.

➕ G7 ✉ Signed off SS129 at Dorgali
🕐 Daily 9–1, 3–7 ♿ None 🎫 Moderate

GOLA SU GORROPPU

www.sardegna-ambiente.it

The huge gorge is about 426m (1,400ft) deep and 8km (4.8 miles) long. Called Europe's Grand Canyon, it follows the Rio Flumineddu river; hiking to it is an arduous all-day venture.

➕ G8 ✉ 10km (6 miles) south of Dorgali
🕐 Best spring and summer; avoid periods of high water ♿ None 🎫 Free; excursion expensive

MAMOIADA

www.mamoiada.net

The small town of farmers and herders lies high in the Gennargentu mountains. At the Feast of San Antonio Abate on 16 January, costumed figures dressed in sheepskins, black carved masks and rows of brass cow bells (mamuthones) trudge through town interacting with spectators, driven by colourful issohadores. The tradition dates from pre-Christian times, but some say the issohadores represent the cruel overlords of the Spanish period. The Museo delle Maschere Mediterranee houses fine examples

Cattedrale di Santa Maria delle Neve, Núoro (left); the town of Dorgali (above)

of these costumes and others from around the Mediterranean.

✠ F7 ⊠ South of Núoro off SS389 ☎ Museo: 0784 569 018 ⏰ Museo: Tue–Sun 9–1, 3–7 (Jul–Sep daily) 🍴 Several 🚆 Frequent service from Núoro Central Station except Sun ♿ Good 💰 Inexpensive

NÚORO

Atop a mountain ridge, Núoro has scarcely a level area. The 19th-century neoclassical cathedral of Santa Maria della Neve sits on a cliff, with magnificent views from the *piazza* beside it. The Museo dell'Arte della Provincia di Núoro features 20th-century and contemporary art, and Museo Deleddiano is the childhood home of Nobel Prize (1926) writer Grazia Deledda. In addition to the costume museum the National Archaeological Museum has excellent collections, from mammalian fossils to Neolithic artefacts.

✠ F7 ⊠ SP129 southwest of Ólbia ☎ 0784 38777 🍴 Numerous 🚆 Frequent service from Ólbia airport ♿ Few

NÚORO: MUSEO DELLA VITA

Although only a small fraction of its thousands of Sardinian costumes and decorative art are currently displayed, this museum is breathtaking. Dozens of authentic dresses and men's suits are shown on models, complete with jewellery and accessories just as they were when worn by their original owners at weddings, funerals and festivals. The finesse of the embroidery, lace and other needlework is astonishing. Also displayed are children's clothes, baptismal dresses, filigree jewellery, household and religious items and an entire gallery of traditional masks.

✠ F7 ⊠ Via A. Mereu 56 ☎ 0784 257 035 ⏰ Oct–15 Jun daily 9–1, 3–7; 16 Jun–Sep 9–8 ♿ Very good 💰 Inexpensive

OLIENA

Stone-paved streets wind up from Chiesa Santa Maria into a tangle of lanes where the unique local architectural styles–recessed balconies, plant-filled courtyards

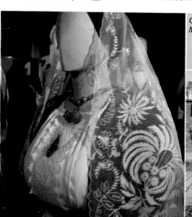

Costumes displayed in the Museo della Vita, Núoro

Sculpture in Piazza Sebastiano, Núoro

and quirky chimneys—are highlighted by occasional wall murals and pictorial tiles in Piazza Berlunguer. Inside the church is an extraordinary presepio with the Holy Family, wise men, shepherds and townspeople hand-crafted by a local ceramic artist—bring an electric torch to see details. The older women here still dress in long black skirts and shawls.

➕ G7 ✉ 7km (4 miles) southeast of Núoro 🍴 Few 🚌 From Núoro and Dorgali ♿ Few ❓ Market Sat 7–2

ORGOSOLO

Resistant to government incursions into what villagers consider their prerogatives, the fiercely independent people of the Barbagia region have created more than 150 murals on the walls of this village, most of which protest social and political issues. (This local independence has also resulted in bullet holes in traffic signs and in the front of the town hall.) Some of the paintings in this open-air art gallery are in the realist style; others seem Picasso-inspired, touching on everything from protests of the Iraq war and outrage over greedy landlords to religious and nature themes. The Feast of the Assumption (15 August) features equestrians and local costumes.

➕ G7 ✉ South of Núoro and Oliena 🍴 Few 🚌 Frequent service from Núoro ♿ Few, but most murals are easily seen

S'ENA E THOMES

Locally called *tombe di giganti*, meaning giant's tombs, these long burial chamber tombs dating from the early Bronze Age feature a large carved central stele (standing stone) with a small circular opening in front, flanked by standing stones on either side. Behind, the rectangular stones of this unusually well-preserved tomb create a passage capped with other flat stones, originally covered with soil.

➕ G7 ✉ On SS129 between Núoro and Dorgali 🕐 Open access ♿ None 💷 Free

Detail of one of many murals displayed in Orgosolo

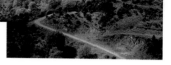

The Gennargentu

Tortuous hairpin roads climb through some of Sardinia's most rugged and beautiful interior mountains with breathtaking views.

DISTANCE: 70km (43.5 miles)   **ALLOW:** a day with stops

START

NÚORO
🔲 F7

🚌

❶ Leave Núoro on Via Giovanni XXIII, bearing right onto Via Aspromonte and right again onto the SS129, all the while following signs to Oliena.

🚌

❷ Follow the SS129 along the steep slope of Monte Ortabene, high above the valley, turning right onto the SP22, signposted Oliena.

🚌

❸ Cross the river and climb to Oliena (▷ 86), stopping to stroll its steep streets and admire its flower-decked courtyards and balconies.

🚌

❹ A side trip 7km (4 miles) east on the SP46, signposted 'Dorgali', leads to Su Gologone, a good stop for lunch or shopping at its gallery of local artists and artisans (▷ 89).

END

NÚORO
🔲 F7

🚌

❽ Visit the Museo delle Maschere Mediterranee (▷ 85) before leaving Mamoiada on Via Núoro. Turn right onto the SS389 to return to Núoro.

🚌

❼ Take time to explore Orgosolo (▷ 87) and admire its wall murals before leaving town on the SP22 towards Mamoiada.

🚌

❻ After about 7km (4 miles), turn left onto the SP58, signposted 'Orgosolo' (for a more thrilling approach, you can follow the tortuous SP22 directly from Oliena).

🚌

❺ Backtrack to Oliena. Leave Oliena on Via Monni.

DRIVE

THE EAST

Shopping

FALEGNAMERIA ARTIGIANA DI DOMENICO CUGUSI

Magnificent hand-carved wedding chests in authentic designs, produced in the same way as the 18th-century Barbaricina chests you can see displayed in museums.

🏠 F8 ✉ Via Roma 33, Gavoi ☎ 0784 52000
🚌 From Núoro

ISOLA

The Istituto Sardo Organizzazione Lavoro Artigiano is dedicated to preserving the island's art and craft heritage. The range of locally produced goods sold here includes foods, clothing, ceramics and hand-weaving, knives and wooden ware. Each piece is authenticated.

🏠 F7 ✉ Corso Garibaldi 58, Núoro ☎ 078 433 581

MUSEO DELLE MASCHERE MEDITERRANEE

Hand-carved replicas of traditional *mamuthone* and other masks.

SARDINIAN STYLE

Contemporary Sardinian artists continue to interpret motifs and techniques from their rich heritage, working in traditional media with traditional themes, but continually creating new styles from these influences. Nowhere is this phenomenon seen more vividly that in the gallery at Su Gologone (▷ right).

🏠 F7 ✉ Piazza Europa 15, Mamoiada ☎ 0784 569 018

ROSAURA SANNA CERAMICHE

The ceramicist Rosaura Sanna has a degree in sculpture and today creates contemporary tableware, vases and decorative items.

🏠 F7 ✉ Strada F, Zona Industriale Prato Sardo Lotto 71, Núoro ☎ 0784 294 035

SU GOLOGONE

Paintings, sculpture, jewellery, textiles, pottery, baskets, masks and wooden chests are a few of the crafts beautifully displayed in this gallery of top Sardinian artists and craftsmen.

🏠 G7 ✉ Oliena ☎ 0784 287 512

Entertainment and Activities

ARGONAUTA

www.argonauta.it
Professionally guided snorkelling tours, dives to sea caves and World War II shipwrecks, plus PADI courses at all levels.

🏠 H7 ✉ Via dei Lecci 10, Cala Gonone ☎ 0784 93046
🕐 By reservation only

BOCA CHICA

A lively bar and disco, often with nationally known DJs, on the edge of town near the SP58 intersection.

🏠 F7 ✉ Via Mughina 94, Núoro ☎ 329 312 0010
🕐 Thu–Sun from 10pm

COOPERATIVA GHIVINE

www.ghivine.com/excursions. htm
Walking excursions throughout the Gulf of Orosei and Gennargentu region; rock climbing, canyon exploration, one- and two-day tented hikes and mountain trips by four-wheel-drive vehicles.

🏠 H7 ✉ Via Lamármora 69, Dorgali ☎ 0784 96721
🕐 By reservation only

COOPERATIVA GORROPU

www.gorropu.com
Guided day hikes and walks to the Gola Su Gorroppu, also caving and canyoning, cooking courses and botanical field trips.

🏠 G8 ✉ Via Sa Preda Lada 2, Urzulei ☎ 0782 649 282
🕐 By reservation only

Restaurants

AI MONTI DEL GENNARGENTU (€€)

www.aimontidelgennargentu.com

Lying 5km (3 miles) from Orgosolo, this well-regarded rustic restaurant in an *albergo* (inn) serves pasta dishes that are a notch above the usual, and the roasted local meats are excellent.

➕ F7 ✉ Località Settiles, Orgosolo ☎ 0784 402 374, 339 701 3183 ⏰ Daily lunch and dinner

LA CAMPAGNOLA (€–€€)

www.lacampagnola.net

Popular with the locals, this restaurant is known for its grilled local meats and for pizza baked in a wood oven. In good weather the dining room spills onto a terrace overlooking the gardens.

➕ F7 ✉ Via Satta 2a, Mamoiada ☎ 0784 56396 ⏰ Daily lunch and dinner

COLIBRI (€–€€)

Sample Sardinian favourites using only the best of local meats, pastas, cheeses and olives. The *su sirboni* (local wild boar) is outstanding.

➕ H7 ✉ Via Gramcsci

14, Dorgali ☎ 0784 96054 ⏰ Mon–Sat 12–3, 7.30–11

I GIARDINI DI CALA GINEPRO (€€€)

www.calaginepro.com

Dishes such as *carpaccio* of salmon, sea scallops in Mornay sauce and seafood risotto are served in an upscale resort environment.

➕ H7 ✉ Viale Cala Ginepro 76, Orosei ☎ 0784 91047

IL PESCATORE (€€€)

Fine dining on the coast, specializing in serving only the freshest fish and seafood cooked in Mediterranean styles, although other dishes are available, too. In warm weather, dine outside. Bookings are advisable.

➕ H7 ✉ Via Acqua Dolce, Cala Gonone ☎ 0784 93174 ⏰ Daily 12–3, 7.30–11 🚌 From Núoro and Dorgali

SU GOLOGONE

Recognized as one of the most authentic restaurants on the island, Su Gologone's (€€–€€€) cuisine is based on recipes handed down through the generations. They will even give tips on preparation of local specialities such as *pane frattau* (local flat bread that is prepared in a unique way).

➕ G7 ✉ Oliena, just off the Núoro–Oliena road ☎ 0784 287 512; www.sugolone.it ⏰ Apr–Sep daily lunch and dinner

RISTORANTE ALBERGO SANT'ELENE (€€)

From the terrace of this hillside restaurant there are glorious views and the regional cuisine is splendid.

➕ G7 ✉ Località Sant'Elena, 3km off the SS125 from Dorgali ☎ 0784 94572 ⏰ Tue–Sun lunch and dinner; closed Jan

RISTORANTE DON CHISCIOTTE (€€)

www.ristorantedonchisciotte.org

Their classic Sardinian cuisine, such as *spaghetti alla bottarga* (with mullet roe), *gnocchetti sarde*, *pane frattau* and roasted *calamari*—all prepared with care and nicely presented—is highly regarded and draws diners in from far and wide.

➕ F7 ✉ Piazza Vittorio Veneto 31, Núoro ☎ 0784 257061 ⏰ Tue–Sun lunch and dinner

RISTORANTE GRILLO (€–€€)

www.grillohotel.it

This dining room in central Núoro has been a consistent winner of regional dining awards. The menu goes beyond the usual local fare, with delicate home-made pasta, and meat dishes incorporating fresh seasonal vegetables.

➕ F7 ✉ Via Monsignor Melas 14, Núoro ☎ 0784 386 68 ⏰ Daily lunch and dinner

Long white beaches between high, rocky headlands, possibly the best of all the Nuraghi, a Phoenician/Roman city and the castellated heights of Cágliari combine to make the south 'Sardinia in a nutshell'.

9

10

Punta Funtánas

S António
di Santadí

Punta de s'Achívoni

Golfo di Porto Pistis

Pistis

Porto Palma

Murta

Marina di
Arbus

Pardu Atzei

Punta di Tremolia

Punta Campu Sali

11

Piscinas

785
Monte
Arcuentu

Piccalinna

Bocca de Riu Piscina

Costa Verde

Bau

Gúspini
Árbus

197

Iblu

Pabillónis

San Gavino
Monreale

197

Nuraghe Su
Nuraxi

Genuri

Turri

Ussaramanna
Siddi

Lunamatrona

Sárdara

E25 131

Sanlu

Fur

Porto Pischera

126

Terramaistus

Gonnosfanádiga

196

Villacidro

Samas

Capo Pécora

Parco geominerario
storico ed ambientale
della Sardegna

Fluminimaggiore

1236
Punta Perda
de sa Mesa

Torrente Leni

Serramanna

196

Villasor

San Nicolao

F l u m i n e s e

910

12

Cala Doméstica

Lago
Monteponi

Masua

Lago Ponta
Gennarta

Porto di Nébida

Golfo di Gonnesa

Nébida

San Benedetto

906
Punta San Michele

Punta Cuccurdoni
Mannu

Iglésias

Domusnóvas

130

293

Vallermosa

Decimoputzu

130 Villa Speciossa

Porto Páglia

Gonnesa

126

Cíxerri

Silíqua

Uta

Capo Altano
o Giordano

Bacu Abis

Villamassargia

13

Isola Piana

Portoscuso

Punta delle Oche

Punta
Tabarchina

Nuraxi
Figus

Barbusi

Sirri

Parco geominerario
storico ed ambientale
della Sardegna

948
Monte Arcosu

Lago di
Medau
Zirimilis

Capo Sándalo

Tonnare

Paringianu

126

Ísola di San Pietro

Carloforte

la Caletta

Punta
di Girin

Matzáccara

Carbónia

Narcao

Acquacadda

Perdáxius

293

Núxis

1105
Monte Tiríccu

Capoterr

Riserva
Naturale Foresta
di Monte Arcosu

14

Punta delle Colonne
Punta Maggiore

Calasetta

126d

S Antíoco

San Giovanni Suérgiu

Lago di
Monte Pranu

Giba

Santadi

San Giórgi
Villa San Piet

Punta Caragoli

Ísola di
Sant'Antíoco

Golfo di Pálmas

195

Masainas

Striólfi

Pul

Colonia

Cala sa Barracca

Stagno
Baiocca

Sant' Anna
Arresi

Stagno de
is Brebéis

is Pillonis

195

Teulada

Santa Margherita

Punta Grossa
la Fazenda
Capo Sperone

Punta Menga

Sant' Isidoro

Costa del Sud

Domus de
Maria

195

Chia

Forte Villag

Ísla la Vacca

Punta Zaffaraneddu

Punta di Cala Piombo

Punta di
onnara

Capo
Malfatano

Porto Campana

Capo
Spartivento

15

Ísla il Toro

Capo Teulada

A   **B**   **C**   **D**

Cágliari

THE SOUTH ★ TOP 25

HIGHLIGHTS

● The old streets of Castello
● Bastione di Saint Remy
● Museo Archeológico
● Crypts and Pisan pulpit in the cathedral

TIP

● The lifts behind Santa Chiara, at Bastione di Saint Remy and off Piazza Palazzo, save a lot of climbing.

D. H. Lawrence may have stretched the point a bit in calling the Sardinian capital a 'white Jerusalem', but its walls and bastions rising in layers from the Bay Of Angels are unquestionably impressive.

Romans to Renzo Piano More than any other Sardinian city, Cágliari shows the influences of the diverse cultures that have come and gone. Its population, traditions and especially its architecture reflect its role as an historic melting pot. Witness the town hall, a heady blend of Aragonese Gothic and Liberty (art nouveau) style. From the stately neoclassical arcades facing the port to the severe bastions, medieval towers and baroque churches of Castello and the modernist Palazzo del CIS, designed by Piano, the city's charm lies in its infinite variety.

Clockwise from far left: Spectacular views from Bastione di Saint Remy; shuttered windows and ornate balconies, typical of the Villanova district; remains of a Roman amphitheatre; the Sardinian flag flying outside the town hall in Palazzo Comunale; view over the city from the Castello district

THE BASICS

www.visit-cagliari.it
✚ E13
✉ On the south coast
☎ 070 669 255
🍴 Plentiful
🛳 Tirrenia from Naples, Palermo and Trapani
❓ CTM city transit maps available from tourist offices

Museo Archeológico
www.archeocaor.beniculturali.it
✉ Piazza Arsenale
☎ 070 655 911
🕐 Tue–Sun 9–8
🍴 Café (€–€€)
🚌 Circolare 7
♿ Very good
🎫 Moderate

Lofty fortress Several sights are concentrated in the sloping tangle of Castello's stone streets, once the stronghold of the Pisans and Genovese, and briefly home to the Savoy royal family. Although most of its walls were destroyed in the 1860s when life moved into the new waterfront Marina quarter, the medieval Elephant Tower and others still stand. Admire the city from the Bastione di Saint Remy, a spacious terrace reached by a grand staircase from Piazza Costituzione.

Art and history At the other end of Castello, past the Cattedrale Santa Maria, is Cittadella dei Musei. The Museo Archeológico displays ancient artefacts in well-designed galleries and the art museum holds precious *retablos* (carved painted altars) from destroyed churches.

Ísola di Sant'Antíoco & Ísola di San Pietro

TOP 25

Parco Archeológico, Sant'Antíoco (left); Carloforte on San Pietro (right)

THE BASICS

www.archeotur.it

🔟 B14/A13

✉ Off the southwest coast

🍽 Several

🚌 From Iglésias

♿ Antiquarium good; archaeological sites few

⛴ Ferries connect Calasetta, on Sant'Antíoco, to Ísola di San Pietro

Parco Archeológico

✉ Via S. Moscati, Sant'Antíoco

☎ 0781 800 596; www.archeotur.it

🕐 Museum and *tophet* daily 9–7; Villaggio Ipogeo Apr–Sep 9–8; 1–15 Oct 9–1, 3.30–8; 16 Oct–Mar 9.30–1, 3–6

HIGHLIGHTS

● Archeological museum
● Villaggio Ipogeo, where 20th-century families made their homes in tombs of the Punic era
● Catacombs beneath the Basilica di S.Antíoco Martire

Sant'Antíoco is a microcosm of all those who have inhabited or controlled Sardinia, while on San Pietro it's all about Genoa.

Sant'Antíoco Begin at the Antiquarium museum, for its neolithic, Byzantine, Phoenician and Roman artefacts and interactive map identifying the island's prehistoric sites. Much of the collection is from the *tophet*, shown and interpreted to make the site more comprehensible. Climb to the *tophet* itself, where eighth-century BC Phoenicians, and later Carthaginians, buried the cremated remains of children in urns marked by steles. After walking among the niches, follow the path to the little ethnographic museum, where a guided tour explores the necropolis carved into bedrock.

Castle and catacombs The castle above began as a Punic fort built on a Nuraghic tower from about 1800BC. In 1812 the Savoys continued the project with the current fort. More Phoenician-Punic connected tombs, later turned into catacombs, lie under the Basilica di Sant'Antíoco Martire below the castle. The little museum behind the church is worth a visit.

San Pietro At first approach it might be easy to mistake Carloforte, on Ísola di San Pietro, for part of the Ligurian coast. It was settled by Genoese fishermen in the 1700s, and their dialect is still spoken there. Tour boats explore the rock formations of Punta delle Colonne.

Remains of Roman columns (left), mosaics (middle) and an amphitheatre (right)

Nora

On a peninsula jutting into the sea, Nora has known all the major Mediterranean cultures. Phoenicians, Carthaginians and Romans once lived in this coastal city.

Phoenician founders Nora was probably first settled by Nuraghic peoples, but by the first millennium BC Phoenician traders from North Africa began trading here. They settled, pushing further inland, and erecting a temple to fertility goddess Tanit. Carthaginians eventually supplanted the Phoenicians until they themselves were ejected by the Romans in 238BC. For the next seven centuries Nora remained an important city, until attacks by pirates and Saracens from North Africa led to its abandonment.

Roman remains Today Nora is a huge open-air museum of Sardinian antiquity. While most is of Roman origin, traces of its Phoenician past are still visible. The streets and substantial parts of the walls of buildings remain. Huge segments of the toppled walls of Roman baths tower over the street, and the interior of the Roman theatre is so well preserved that it is used for summer performances. Some reports claim as much as a third of Nora is under the sea, but studies show only 4m (12ft) of subsidence over the past two millennia, so little of the city is now believed to lie below the water. Large portions are, however, buried beneath a derelict military base. A beautiful beach connects Nora to the Byzantine-style church of Sant'Efisio built in 1089 where the saint was beheaded by Romans in AD303.

THE BASICS

🚻 E14
✉️ Pula, 30km (18.5 miles) south of Cágliari
🕐 Daily 9–7.30
🍴 Restaurant and bar nearby at Sant'Efisio
🚌 Shuttle from Pula
♿ Few; paths are rough
💰 Moderate

San Efisio
☎ 340 4851 860
🕐 Sat 2.30–5.30, Sun 10–12, 2.30–5.30

HIGHLIGHTS

● Roman theatre
● Roman baths
● Temple of Tanit
● Church of Sant'Efisio

TIPS

● Wear comfortable walking shoes for manoeuvring over rough stone streets.
● Allow two hours to see the site.

THE SOUTH

★ **TOP 25**

TOP 25

Nuraghe Su Nuraxi

Various views of the Nuraghe cone tower at Su Naraxi

THE BASICS

www.comunebarumini.it

🔳 E10

✉ Viale Su Nuraxi, Barúmini

☎ 070 936 8128

🕐 Daily 9–1 hour before sunset

🍴 Café at site (€)

🚌 Once daily from Cágliari to Barúmini

♿ None

💷 Expensive; includes admission to Casa Zapata museum and Centro di Promozione exhibits

❓ Tours every 30 mins. Visitors must be with a guide inside the Nuraghe tower, but can explore the Nuraghic village on their own

HIGHLIGHTS

● Exploring inside the walls and towers
● The village of *capane* (round house) walls
● Nuraghe tower foundations at Casa Zapata
● Archaeological finds from the Nuraghe

If you can only see one Nuraghic tower and village while in Sardinia, make it this UNESCO World Heritage Site, which was cited as one of the best restorations in the Mediterranean.

Skilled builders While dry-stone *thalos* (stacked) domes are found elsewhere, only in Sardinia were they used to build towers three floors high, as here. The walls are about 2m (6ft) thick, and inside spiral stairways connect the levels, showing the astonishing sophistication of the builders. A rare wooden timber in the walls gave a carbon date of 1500BC. Outer towers were built in the 11th or 12th century BC.

Look inside Casa Zapata, in Barúmini, might look like the usual 16th-century manor house, but a surprise awaited restorers, who discovered that the house was built over a Nuraghe. Its foundations and lower walls are viewed by glass floors, and this is the only place where you can look down into the walls of a Nuraghic tower and see exactly how they were constructed. Display cases show bronzes, beads and terracotta artefacts found at Nuraghe Su Nuraxi, including the miniature of a completed Nuraghic tower showing the balcony at the top.

Museum The ethnographic museum has a section on traditional reed musical instruments, displays showing how local pasta is made, traditional tools and household implements.

Fortezza Vecchia (left); boats rest in Villasimíus harbour (right)

Villasimíus and Costa Rei

Were it not for the lovely beaches elsewhere on the island, it would seem unfair for one town to be surrounded by so many strands of perfect sand and turquoise water.

Beaches and more In addition to being a popular beach resort, Villasimíus is a town with a real life of its own. In season, its promenade of shops, cafés and restaurants occupy tourists between trips to the beaches of Timi Ama, Simius Playa and Spiaggia del Riso. The latter gets its name (*riso* means rice) from the tiny particles of sea-worn white quartz that form its sand. Spiaggia Portu Giuncu separates the sea from the Notteri Marsh lagoon, home to pink flamingos. The excellent archaeological museum displays Roman and Phoenician artefacts from local sites and salvage from a 16th-century Spanish ship, wrecked off the coast.

High headland Capo Carbonara and its small offshore islands are protected as a nature reserve, and are reached by boats from the marina. Capo Carbonara juts southward in a headland, the island's most southeasterly point. After passing the marina and Fortezza Vecchia, a 17th-century tower, the road ends with views of a lighthouse and old quarry house, far below.

Costa Rei To the north is the Costa Rei, a countryside of sheep pastures and olive and almond groves that drops to beautiful golden sand beaches with very little development.

THE BASICS

➕ G14/G13
✉ 50km (31 miles) southwest of Cágliari
🍴 Plentiful
🚌 From Cágliari
♿ Few

Museo Archaeológico
✉ Via A. Frau 5
☎ 070 793 0290
🕐 15 Jun–15 Sep Tue–Sat 10–1, 9–12; 16 Sep–14 Jun Tue–Sat 10–1, also Fri–Sun 5–7

Fortezza Vecchia
✉ Marina
🕐 15 Jun–Jul Mon–Sat 10–1, 6–9; Aug–15 Sep Mon–Sat 10–1, 5–8

HIGHLIGHTS

● Incomparable beaches
● Drive along the Costa Rei
● Snorkelling off Capo Carbonara

More to See

BARÚMINI: PARCO SARDEGNA IN MINIATURA

www.sardegnainminiatura.it

Scale replicas of major island buildings include a Nuraghic village, a rare chance to see completed buildings. Paths wind through the park, which also has a planetarium, astronomical museum and riverboat rides for children.

✚ E10 ✉ Viale Su Nuraxi, Barúmini
☎ 070 936 1004 🕐 Apr–Oct daily 10–5
🍽 Café (€–€€) 🚌 Once a day from Cágliari 🛗 Very good 💰 Expensive

CARBÓNIA

Founded in 1938 by the Italian Facist government to develop local coal mining, Carbonia has a legacy of modernist/rationalist architecture, including the city hall, Piazza Roma, theatre and San Ponziano church. In contrast are prehistoric *domus de janas* Monte Crobu, Necropoli di Cannas di Sottos and the Phoenician-Punic ruins on Monte Sirai. Treasures from those excavations are displayed in the Museo Archeológico Villa Sulcis.

✚ C13 ✉ SS126, west of Cágliari
🍽 Several 🚌 From Cágliari 🛗 Few

COSTA DEL SUD

South of Pula, sandy beaches hide in coves between headlands with round Spanish towers. The SP71 winds through this spectacular scenery of promontories and islands, the sea almost constantly in view. Inland, the mountain WWF reserve of Monte Arcosu protects birds, wild boar and indigenous deer.

✚ D15 ✉ SP71, southwest of Cágliari
🍽 In beach resorts 🛗 Few

COSTA VERDE

West of Arborea, a plain separates the sea and mountains and along the shore lie some of Sardinia's finest and least-used beaches. A twisting road climbs north from Guspini, turning south to the Spiaggia della Costa Verde. Behind the beaches lie the Dune di Scivu, among Europe's tallest dunes.

✚ C11 ✉ South of Oristano 🛗 None

One of 20 beaches on the Costa del Sud

GIARA DI GESTURI

Between Barúmini and Albagiara, north of Tuili, a high basaltic plateau is home to about 700 small wild horses and the red long-horned cattle so favoured on island tables. This unsettled area of *macchia* and cork oak is a popular place for nature walks.

➕ E10 ✉ East of Oristano ♿ None

IGLÉSIAS

www.igeaminiere.it

Climb the narrow streets of the old city, past the 13th-century Gothic cathedral of Santa Chiara, to reach the promenade along its defensive walls. Derelict mining operations line the road to the west; it is best to reserve ahead to tour the mines of Porto Flavia, where an ingenious system transferred ore from inside the mountain to cargo ships. The Museo dell'Arte Mineraria displays 200 years of mining equipment and actual training tunnels.

➕ C12 ✉ West of Cágliari ☎ Mining

Museum: 0781 491 300 🕐 Museum Jun Sat–Sun 6–8, Jul–Sep Sat–Sun 7–9

🍴 Several 🚌 From Cágliari ♿ Few

POETTO

The 13km (9.5-mile) stretch of golden sand (some imported from the Sahara) is one of the island's longest, cooled by northwesterly breezes. Restaurants, snack bars, cafés and amusements line the promenade, and behind stretches the Stagno di Molentargius, a lagoon where flamingos nest.

➕ E13 ✉ Just east of Cágliari 🍴 Plentiful

🚌 P, PF, PQ from Piazza Matteoti ♿ Good

SAN SPERATE

Artist Pinuccio Sciola began painting murals in 1968, followed by Italian and foreign artists, and today San Sperate is one of Sardinia's 'painted towns'. Many are on Via Monasterio, parallel to Via Risorgimento and Via Ararei, where an entire house has been decorated by various artists.

➕ E12 ✉ 20km (12.5 miles) northwest of Cágliari 🍴 Café (€) ♿ Good

Brightly coloured beach huts at Poetto beach

Wild ponies graze on the Giara di Gesturi

Cágliari's Castello

The historic heart of Cágliari (▷ 94–95), the Castello, crowns a hill above the harbour set apart by its bastions.

DISTANCE: 1.6km (1 miles) **ALLOW:** 1.5 hours with stops, plus museums

START

CHIESA DI SANTA CHIARA
 b2 🚌 Circolare 7

END

PIAZZA ARSENALE
b1 🚌 Circolare 7 or Line 6

❶ Take the lift behind the Chiesa di Santa Chiara and at the top walk right to Torre dell'Elefante. Look up to see the carved stone elephant that gives the tower its name.

❷ Go through the gate and turn left to the Terrazza Bastione di Santa Croce for sweeping views over the city. Backtrack through the tower and turn left onto Via Università.

❸ Follow Via Università; climb to Bastione di Saint Remy for views over the harbour, Villanova quarter and to Basilica di Nostra Signora di Bonaria.

❹ Climb the steps on your left to the upper level. Follow Via Fossario to the Duomo, filled with treasures including the original pulpit from the Duomo in Pisa.

❼ Go through the arch at the far side into Piazza Arsenale to the Cittadella dei Musei, with the Museo Archeológico and an art museum.

❻ At the end of the palace make a short detour to the right to admire the views before continuing on Via Pietro Martini past the little church of Santa Lucia into Piazza Indipendenza. Ahead is the medieval Torre di San Pancrazio.

❺ Continue into Piazza Palazzo, passing the Palazzo Arcivescovile (archbishop's palace) and the long facade of the Palazzo Regio, home to the Savoy Royal family during Napoleon's capture of Turin.

WALK

THE SOUTH

Cágliari to Villasimíus

From the calm waters of the Gulf of Angels to Sardinia's southeast point, with scenic headlands and stunning beaches in between.

DISTANCE: 70km (43.5 miles) **ALLOW:** half day, full day with beach stops

START

CÁGLIARI
✚ E13

1 From the port in Cágliari, head east along the shore, following signs to Poetta, a long stretch of beaches lined with *cabanas* and beachside amusements.

2 Go right at the roundabout and continue past farm stands selling fresh fruit in summer, to Nuraghe Diana in Capitana, transformed into a watch tower in World War II.

3 Continue on the coastal road, now twisting and turning as it climbs over scenic headlands, to Torre delle Stelle; a sidetrack right leads to a nice beach.

4 Continue to Solánus, about 5km (3 miles) farther on, turning right into the bougainvillea-draped resort town where the hotels are all within walking distance of the long beach.

END

VILLASIMÍUS
✚ G14

7 Take the road left from the marina, passing the 17th-century Fortezza Vecchia (▷ 99), to the end of the point. Return to the marina and go straight ahead into Villasimíus.

6 Turn right, following signs to Capo Carbonara, and bearing right again to the marina at Porto Villasimíus, where boats leave for snorkelling and island beaches.

5 Return to the coast road, which begins a series of hairpin turns to ascend another headland, this one with a Spanish tower at its point. About 5km (3 miles) farther on is an overlook with views of Capo Carbonara and the white crescent of Campus beach below.

Shopping

ANTIQUARIUM

The museum shop carries beautiful silver jewellery replicating or inspired by ancient artefacts, along with books on historical sights and themes.
🔲 B14 ✉ Via S. Moscati, Sant'Antíoco ☎ 0781 800 596

ARGIOLAS WINERY

www.argiolas.it
One of the finest wineries on the island, Argiolas has more than 250ha (620 acres) of vines that produce reds, whites and a dessert wine from very ripe Malvesia and Nasco grapes. Argiolas also makes Grappa di Turriga; they offer tastings, sales and tours.
🔲 E12 ✉ Via Roma 28, Serdiana, about 20km (12.5 miles) north of Cágliari ☎ 070 740 606

BOB ART

The little gallery shop sells quirky, original decorative and useful artworks in buoyant designs and colours.
🔲 c2 ✉ Via Torino 12, Cágliari ☎ 399 389 5530

ISCA E MURAS

Sardinian honey and honey-based sweets, along with soaps and other cosmetics based on products from local hives.
🔲 E10 ✉ Via IV Novembre 3, Barúmini ☎ 070 936 8086

ISOLA

This well respected crafts institute carries the works of Sardinia's best artists and artisans. It's about 300m (330 yards) beyond the market at San Benedetto, but worth the trip.
🔲 E13 ✉ Via Bacaredda 176–8, Cágliari ☎ 070 492 756 🚌 1, 6

SAN BENEDETTO MARKET

Cagliari's main food market fills two floors—and often the street—with the freshest products of Sardinian land and waters. It is impossible not to sample the local cheeses offered, and the market is a less expensive source of packaged food gifts than gourmet shops.
🔲 E13 ✉ Between Via Cocco Ortu and Via Bacaredda, Cágliari 🕐 Every morning and all day Sat 🚌 1, 6

MARKETS

Cágliari features street markets where collectors and dealers gather nearly every Sunday morning during good weather to buy and sell everything from serious antiques to bric-a-brac:

● First Sunday of the month at Piazza Giovanni XXIII (northeast of the centre 🚌 1, 3, 29)
● Second Sunday of the month at Piazza Carlo Alberto (Castello)
● Third Sunday of the month at Piazza Galilei (Villanova 🚌 1)

SAPORI DI SARDEGNA

www.saporidisardegna.com
Find traditional foods such as *pane carrasau* (flat bread), *bottarga* (mullet roe), marmalades and honeys, *mallared- dus* (pasta) and a big selection of local cheeses including pecorino fresh, semi-aged and aged. Also fine hand-woven baskets and traditional pottery.
🔲 b3 ✉ Vico dei Mille 1 (off Via Roma), Cágliari ☎ 070 684 8747 🕐 Oct–Apr Mon–Sat 9–1.30, 3.30–8.30; May–Sep 9–8.30

S'ARGIDDA DI FAUSTO CABONI

www.zafferanosargidda.com
Sardinia is one of the few places where high-quality saffron grows, and in November, when these precious crocuses bloom, you can visit the farm to see them picked, threads extracted from each blossom and 'polished' in olive oil—all by hand. Buy saffron in handcrafted ceramic and terracotta pots.
🔲 D11 ✉ SS197, San Gavino Monreale (north of Cágliari just off SS131) ☎ 329 371 8772

TERRA ANTICA

Reproductions of the ancient pottery found in Nuraghic sites are hand-made and decorated in this ceramic studio shop.
🔲 E10 ✉ Via Roma 38, Barúmini ☎ 070 936 8089, 320 276 6502

Entertainment and Activities

ANTICO GALEONE

In an Irish pub atmosphere with a Spanish galleon-pirate mix, Antico Galeone frequently has live music at night. It's a good place for lunch, with daily choices, but no printed menu.

🔼 b3 ✉ Via Savoia 1, Cágliari ☎ 347 726 1456 ⏰ Tue–Sun from 11.30am

CAFFÈ LIBARIUM

www.caffelibarium.com
High on Cágliari's bastions, Libarium is a cool, smart bar where locals meet for drinks after work or before dinner for delicious snacks to accompany mixed drinks (a good martini list), beer or wines. Occasional live shows provide music.

🔼 b2 ✉ Via Santa Croce 33–35, Cágliari ☎ 346 522 0212 ⏰ Daily 7.30–11, Sun–Fri 12–3

FIORE DE MAGGIO

Boat tours around the islands of Cavoli and Serpentara and the beaches of Porto Giunco, Is Traias and Simius, with stops for swimming and snorkelling (gear not provided).

🔼 H14 ✉ Porto Villasimíus, Wharf D ☎ 340 486 2894 ⏰ May–Sep daily; by reservation only

JKO'

Disco club popular with locals, except in summer, when the locals leave town to the visitors.

🔼 E13 ✉ Via Contivecchi, Cágliari ☎ No phone ⏰ Thu–Sat midnight–5am

MABY II

www.holidays-in-sardinia.com
Day trips on an historic sailing boat include snorkelling to see fish and a sunken Madonna statue (equipment provided), and beach stops with lunch provided.

🔼 H14 ✉ Porto Villasimíus ☎ 070 891 590 ⏰ Wed, Thu, others by reservation only

PESCATURISMO BARCAS AMIGAS

www.pescaturismosardegna.com
See Ísola di Sant'Antíoco from the sea on a boat excursion that tours the rocky coast and sea caves. Also with fishing, swimming and a lunch of Sardinian specialities.

🔼 B14 ✉ Porti Turistici, Sant'Antíoco ☎ 329 424

7088 or 328 468 1191 ⏰ By reservation only

PESCATURISMO I DUE FRATELLI

www.pescaturismoiduefratelli.com
The 'two brothers' were the first Sant'Antíoco fishermen to introduce tourists to the life of local fishermen, teaching them to use the nets and other gear. Guests also swim from the boat and enjoy the catch for lunch.

🔼 B14 ✉ Lungomare Colombo, Sant'Antíoco ☎ 328 285 5195 ⏰ By reservation only

SARDINIA SAILING

www.sardiniasailing.com
The day-charter sailing ketch *Schatzli II* sails the Sulcis Archipeligo around Ísola di Sant'Antíoco. Lunch is served during the seven-hour voyage.

🔼 B14 ✉ Vico Parrochia 17, Sant'Antíoco ☎ 333 336 7448 ⏰ Sant'Antíoco 9.30–6, Calasetta 10.30–5; by reservation only

TEATRO LIRICO

www.teatroliricodicagliari.it
Cágliari's opera house has a full schedule of concerts, opera and ballet, hosting major international groups and soloists, and its own symphony orchestra and chorus.

🔼 E13 ✉ Via Sant'Alenixedda, Cágliari ☎ 070 408 2230; tickets 070 408 2230, 070 408 2249 ⏰ Concerts Nov–May; opera and ballet Apr–Dec

THE SOUTH

ENTERTAINMENT AND ACTIVITIES

Restaurants

PRICES

Prices are approximate, based on a 3-course meal for one person.

€€€	over €30
€€	€15–€30
€	under €15

CAFÈTTERIA TIFFANY (€)

In a quiet square near Piazza Carlo Felice, this classy tearoom is a fine place to rest feet tired from the cobblestone streets of the old city. Sandwiches are above the ordinary café fare.

➕ b3 ✉ Via Baylle 133, Cágliari ☎ 070 659 216 🕐 Mon–Sat lunch and dinner

MARINA GIÒ (€–€€)

www.marinagio.it

On a sand road along San Giovanni beach, this very popular local restaurant stands out. The *scaloppini impanata alla Marina Giò* is a delicious *parmigiana*-style dish; grilled vegetables are excellent, but main dishes are so bounteous that extras are unnecessary. Most tables overlook the beach, and in summer the dining room spreads out onto the terrace.

➕ G13 ✉ Marina di San Giovanni, Muravera ☎ 333 986 0200 🕐 Tue–Sun 12.30–3, 6–12

RISTORANTE GAZEBO MEDIOEVALE (€€)

Set under the stone vaulting of a medieval palace, this restaurant serves a sophisticated version of the Sardinian classics along with more unusual seafood dishes, such as shrimp in a creamy curry sauce with courgette (zucchini) over spaghetti, or a seafood couscous.

➕ C12 ✉ Via Musio 21, Iglesias ☎ 0781 30871 🕐 Mon–Sat 12–3, 8–10.45

RISTORANTE ITALIA (€–€€)

Since 1921, Ristorante Italia has served Cágliari specialities with an emphasis on seafood. *Fregula con cocciula*, a broth with cockles and clams, is a local favourite, and the spit-roasted suckling pig is just delectable.

➕ b3 ✉ Via Sardegna 30, Cágliari ☎ 070 657 987 🕐 Lunch Mon–Fri, dinner Sat; closed Aug

TINY SIGN, NO MENU

Walking through Villanova you wouldn't notice Dr. Ampex (✉ Via San Giacomo 35 ☎ 070 658 199 🕐 Dinner Mon–Sat). The secret of Cágliari's cognoscenti, the restaurant offers a *prix fixe* of €25 including multiple courses, wine and after-dinner drinks. They choose whatever is freshest each day to create traditional Sardinian dishes. Expect such treats as *bue rossa* (red ox) *carpaccio* with artichokes, mushrooms and rocket (*arugula*). Be sure to reserve ahead.

RISTORANTE RENZO E RITA (€–€€)

www.renzoerita.com

Family owned for generations, the restaurant serves a menu that combines fresh Sardinian ingredients and traditional dishes such as *pane carasau* with wider Mediterranean influences. Grilled tuna and swordfish are excellent. Serves only Sardinian wines.

➕ B14 ✉ Via Nazionale 42, Sant'Antíoco ☎ 0781 800 448 🕐 Thu–Tue 6.30–1am (until 12.30am in winter)

RISTORANTE VILLA DI CHIESA (€–€€)

A warm and hospitable restaurant with artistically presented local dishes. The fresh fish and the grilled fresh vegetables are especially good, and the *sebadas*, traditional pastries filled with fresh cheese, are outstanding.

➕ C12 ✉ Piazza Municipio 9/10, Iglesías ☎ 0781 31641 🕐 Daily lunch and dinner

TRATTORIA GENNARGENTU (€–€€)

A good, inexpensive option with well-prepared local specialities. Close to the centre, one street from Via Roma. The steamed mussels are excellent, served in prodigious portions.

➕ b3 ✉ Via Sardegna 60/c, Cágliari ☎ 070 672 021 🕐 Mon–Sat lunch and dinner

Sardinia has a variety of accommodation to offer travellers. The island's smart luxury hotels are not limited to the northeast corner, Villasimíus and Pula on the southern shore have their share.

Introduction

Lodging options in Sardinia range from modest B&Bs, through *agriturismo* establishments, to city hotels and glamorous resorts in the beach towns of the Costa Smeralda and elsewhere along the coasts. Historic properties converted to hotels are rare, but those few are outstanding.

Booking Ahead

Travellers are perpetually confronted with the question: Should I book ahead and commit to a week at a hotel I haven't seen? Or reserve the first night or two and look around? If you long for a week in the sun and sand, booking ahead and staying in the same place is probably the best plan. But if your dream is to drive around the island to experience different places and see the sights, you should not have difficulty finding places to stay where you get a better opportunity to meet and interact with locals—as long as you avoid the busy season. Be careful, too, in the winter, when many places close down, and even those that are technically open may not be, unless you book in advance. Booking even a few days ahead is easy, either through a hotel's own website, by phone or fax, or through a booking service. Holidays in Sardinia (www.holidays-in-sardinia. com) has a last-minute section that is very helpful and offers money-saving specials.

Plenty of Options

Sardinia offers different lodging options for different tastes and budgets. If nightlife is a priority, choose the popular hotels in the coastal resorts. If travelling with children, look at hotel websites to find play facilities, nearby beaches and entertainment programmes.

AGRITURISMO

If you plan to rent a car and tour the island, the many *agriturismo* properties offer reasonable prices, excellent local food and an experience closer to island life. Normally they come in the form of a cottage or farmhouse and often offer horse riding and excursions.

Accommodation in Sardinia com in many guises: from a luxury h old albergo or tranquil agriturism to chic apartments

Budget Hotels

AGRITURISMO GUTHIDDAI

www.agriturismoguthiddai.com
All eight rooms in this former farm dependency have private entrances and access to gardens. This is a secluded place surrounded by lawns, trees and stony mountain peaks.

➕ G7 ✉ Località Guddithai, Oliena ☎ 0784 286 017 🚍 From Ólbia airport

AGRITURISMO IL MUTO DI GALLURA

www.mutodigallura.com
The stone farmhouse and its cluster of separate bungalows with modern interiors are surrounded by mountains. The farm has a pool, and offers horseback riding on Arabian horses from their own stables.

➕ E3 ✉ Località Fraiga, Aggius ☎ 079 620 559

AGRITURISMO VESSUS

www.vessus.it
Modern buildings are nicely arranged around a large pool and green lawns. Close to town, it offers a relaxing country atmosphere, with its own restaurant; breakfast is included.

➕ B5 ✉ Strada Statale 292,

Alghero ☎ 079 973 6016 🚍 From Alghero-Fertilia Airport

ANTICA DIMORA DEL GRUCCIONE

www.anticadimora.com
This beautiful small hotel is in a 17th-century Spanish-era mansion and adjoining historic buildings, with many antique furnishing. It is located in the medieval part of town and has WiFi in all rooms.

➕ C8 ✉ Via Michelle Obino 31, Santu Lussúrgiu ☎ 0783 552 035 🚍 From Oristano

B&B GAULOS SANT'ANTIOCO

www.gaulosbb.com
A small bed and breakfast close to the monuments; in addition to clean comfortable rooms, guests can enjoy the restful garden and

OUT OF SEASON

If travelling in the winter, when most of the seaside resorts are closed, a good option is bed and breakfast or *agriturismo* farms, where owners live year-round. But don't plan to just show up at the door, since owners may not be there if they are not expecting guests to arrive. Likewise, don't expect a local tourist office to help you find lodgings out of season–they are not likely to be open either.

borrow bicycles.

➕ B14 ✉ Via Goceano 45, Sant'Antioco ☎ 347 049 2487, 347 049 2488

B&B VILLA MARIA LUISA

www.villamarialuisa.eu
The villa's three rooms, directly on Poetto beach can be noisy in summer because of the beach nightlife, but, that said, it's an art deco gem, clean, comfortable and includes breakfast.

➕ E13 ✉ Via Poetto 252, Cágliari ☎ 070 370 454, 347 708 8167 🚍 PF, PQ and QS

LOCANDA IL MELOGRANO

www.locandailmelograno.com
On a superb hillside setting, the newly built guest rooms look out at the castle framed in olive trees. The owners speak fluent English and the trattoria serves original dishes using local seasonal produce from valley farms. Family-friendly.

➕ C7 ✉ Località Tiria 1, Bosa ☎ 339 469 7178 🚍 From Alghero

SU MASSAU

www.agriturismosumassaiu.it
Look for a small sign opposite a lane just outside the village to find this large farm, where walls enclose a grassy patio with a swimming pool. Book dinner, too, since the food is outstanding.

➕ D10 ✉ SP46, Coarvigu, Turri ☎ 078 395 339

WHERE TO STAY BUDGET HOTELS

Mid-Range Hotels

B&B LI ESPI

www.liespi.com
Recently built, the small resort is in Sardinian rural style, about 3km (2 miles) north of Palau. Some of the bright, attractive rooms have sea views. Close to beaches and ferries to the islands, it has a restaurant.

 G2 ✉ SP98 to Ísola dei Gobbiani, Località Li Espi, Palau ☎ 0789 705 032 🚌 Access from SS133, taking the road towards Barrabisa

B&B NIDI DELLA POIANA

www.nididellapoiana.it
Outside of town in an olive grove, the Nidi della Poiana has very attractive rooms in a rural setting with a pool. Breakfast is included. Also apartments close to the centre.

✚ B5 ✉ Località Salondra 50, Alghero ☎ 079 976 894 🚌 From Cágliari

COUNTRY HOTEL IS BENAS

www.isbenaslodge.com
A small hotel northwest of Oristano set In a rural area close to the sea. Surrounded by attractive lawns and gardens with pool, tennis, boules, bike rental and an 18-hole golf course nearby.

✚ C8 ✉ Località Benetudi, SP10, Strada da Mare Putzi Idu, San Vero Milis ☎ 0783 528 022 🕐 May–Sep 🚌 From Oristano

COUNTRY HOTEL MANDRA EDERA

Attractive small resort at a horse-breeding farm and equestrian centre in the hills outside Abbasanta. Most rooms are in bungalows set in gardens. Indoor and outdoor pools, hiking, carriage driving and a restaurant.

✚ D8 ✉ Località Mandra Edera, Abbasanta ☎ 0785 890 222 🚌 Access from SP15 west of Abbsanta interchange

HOTEL CLUB CALA GINEPRO

www.calaginepro.com

Overlooking the Gulf of Orosei, the hotel is a short stroll from its beautiful white sand beach, where lounge chairs, beach volleyball and other activities are available. Multiple pools are scattered around in the nicely landscaped grounds.

✚ H7 ✉ Viale Cala Ginepro 76, Orosei ☎ 0784 91047 🕐 Apr–Oct 🚌 From Ólbia airport

HOTEL GRILLO

Plain, comfortable rooms and an accommodating staff make this a good choice in the centre of town. The restaurant is excellent.

✚ F7 ✉ Via Monsignor Melas 14, Núoro ☎ 0784 38668 🚌 To Núoro 🚌 From Ólbia airport

HOTEL RIVIERA

www.hotelriviera.net
This is a sweet small hotel directly opposite the beach and with outstanding views of the town, the Gulf of Assinara and the castle on the hilltop. Rooms are comfortable and well appointed, with flat-screen TV and phones. Off-road parking is available at the rear, with a lift from the parking level. The restaurant overlooks the main street and beach.

✚ D3 ✉ Lungomare Anglona 1, Castelsardo ☎ 079 470 143 🚌 From Sássari

HOTEL SAN FRANCESCO
www.sanfrancescohotel.com
Former convent where some rooms overlook the cloister of the church of San Francesco. It is the only hotel in the old town centre. Single and double rooms are somewhat spartan, but clean and quiet. Breakfast room in cloister gallery.
🔢 b5 ✉ Via Ambrogio Machin 2, Alghero ☎ 079 980 330 🚌 From Cágliari and Sássari

HOTEL SU NURAXI
www.hotelsunuraxi.it
Visitors to the Barúmini Nuraghe could hardly stay closer, and have the unique opportunity of admiring it lit up at night, just across the road. The rooms of this new contemporary family-run hotel are attractive and comfortable, set around their own small courtyard with the dining room just a few steps away.
🔢 E10 ✉ Viale Su Nuraxi 6, Barúmini ☎ 070 936 8519 🚌 Once daily to and from Cágliari

JANUS HOTEL
www.janushotel.it
At the foot of the hill below the castle, this small designer hotel has attractive rooms and three suites. Proximity to the town beach and sights add to its attraction.
🔢 D3 ✉ Via Roma 85, Castelsardo ☎ 079 479 422 🚌 From Sássari

PETIT HOTEL
www.petit-hotel.it
This modest hotel is perfect for touring Témpio Pausánia. Rooms are attractive but simply furnished and all have a modern bathroom, TV and phone. The Fonte Nova Park is just outside the door.
🔢 F3 ✉ Piazza A. de Gasperi 9–11, Témpio Pausánia ☎ 079 631 134 🚏 To Témpio Pausánia 🚌 From Ólbia

IL QUERCETO
www.ilquerceto.com
In an oak forest with views of the mountains of Gennargentu (the hotel can arrange excursions), the exceptionally large, comfortable rooms are decorated with furniture made by local craftsman. The public areas have art by contemporary regional artists. There are tennis

T HOTEL
The most modern hotel in the city is in a 15-floor glass tower with expansive views over the city and the sea and mountains beyond. Business and fitness centres, free parking, WiFi and high speed in-room internet add to the attraction of its location, opposite the city theatre.
🔢 E13 ✉ Via del Giudicati 1, Cágliari ☎ 070 47400; www.spacehotels.it 🚌 From Piazza Matteotti

courts and a restaurant.
🔢 G7 ✉ Via Lamármora 4, Dorgali ☎ 0784 965 09 🚌 From Núoro and Orosei

SA MOLA
www.samola.it
Sa Mola is an attractive residence hotel of small attached traditional bungalows set in beautiful gardens. The sizeable rooms are quiet and well appointed, and there are both a restaurant and a pizzeria on the property. Close to Oristano, it is well placed for exploring western Sardinia. Reach it by car from the Paulilatino road; the inn is near the intersection, and signposted from there.
🔢 C8 ✉ Via Giardini, Bonárcado ☎ 0783 56588, 0783 56580 🚌 From Oristano

SU GOLOGONE
www.sugologone.it
Sardinian tradition with all mod cons is the key in this inn southeast of Núoro, in the countryside surrounded by oaks and *macchia*. The stony tops of the Sopramonte mountains tower above. Decorated with local art throughout, the inn has nicely appointed rooms, and a restaurant. They arrange guided trekking and excursions to the mountains and archaeological sites.
🔢 G7 ✉ Località Su Gologone, Oliena ☎ 0784 287 512 🕐 May–Oct 🚌 From Núoro

Luxury Hotels

PRICES

Expect to pay more than €200 per night for a double room in a luxury hotel.

COLONNA GRAND HOTEL CAPO TESTA

www.colonnagrandhotel
capotesta.com
Capo Testa's wild wind-carved rocks are a startling contrast to the cool, refined elegance of this super-luxury hotel. On its own promontory overlooking stone-wall-lined paths, multiple pools (some with water-falls) and a white sand beach, the resort has two dining rooms and two bars.

➕ F1 ✉ Località Capo Testa, Santa Teresa di Gallura ☎ 0789 754 950 ⏰ May–Sep 🚌 From Ólbia

FORTE VILLAGE RESORT

www.fortevillage.com
This resort covers extensive parkland and gardens with bungalows and suites overlooking the beach, and rooms in the Hotel Castello. There are several swimming pools, 15 restaurants, tennis courts, playgrounds and a golf practice range, and at the white sand beach are water sports and a diving centre.

➕ E14 ✉ Route SS195, Santa Margarita di Pula ☎ 070 92171; booking 070 921 516 🚌 From Cágliari

GIARDINI DI CALA GINEPRO

www.calaginepro.com
The smartest of the several Cala Ginepro options, Giardini over-looks the Gulf of Orosei, and has a number of large swimming pools. Rooms are spacious and luxuriously furnished, most overlooking the sea from terraces.

➕ H6 ✉ Viale Cala Ginepro 76, Orosei ☎ 0784 91047 ⏰ May–Sep 🚌 From Ólbia airport

GRAND HOTEL IN PORTO CERVO

www.grandhotelinportocervo.it
Just 2km (1 mile) out of town, this hotel has balconies or terraces with most of its rooms, two restaurants, a swimming pool with panoramic

VILLA LAS TRONAS

Finding luxury hotels that are not international chains is difficult in Sardinia, where development money has gone to new resorts since the 1970s. So this *palazzo* on its own little point above the sea is all the more alluring. Suites are opulent, and the service is flawless and gracious. Its first owners entertained royalty here, and the present ones make guests feel royal.

➕ B5 ✉ Lungomare Valencia 1, Alghero ☎ 079 981 818; www.villalastronas. com 🚌 From Sássari and Cágliari

views, a fitness centre and a sunbathing area on a nearby beach.

➕ H2 ✉ Località Cala Granu, Porto Cervo ☎ 0789 91533 ⏰ May–Sep 🚌 From Ólbia

HOTEL COLONNA PEVERO

www.colonnapeverohotel.it
The size, modern elegance, gardens, fountains and waterfall at this luxury hotel on a hillside overlooking the town create more of a villa experience than other Porto Cervo hotels. The buildings wrap nicely around its green areas and five pools (one reserved for children, another with hydro-massage). Rooms are a bit small, but all have a veranda or terrace.

➕ H2 ✉ Località Golfo de Perero ☎ 0789 907 009 ⏰ May–Sep 🚌 From Ólbia

HOTEL SAN PANTALEO—PETRA SEGRETA RESORT

www.petrasegretaresort.com
This small resort in the hills overlooking the Gulf of Arzachena is known for its wellness spa. Rooms are in typical regional houses, throughout the forested grounds, along with a restaurant, wine bar and piano bar.

➕ G3 ✉ Strada di Buddeo, Buddeo, San Pantaleo ☎ 0789 183 1365, 346 152 1187 ⏰ Apr–Oct

The following section will help plan your trip to Sardinia. You'll find advice on when to go, getting there and getting around, along with practical information for travelling around this lovely island.

Planning Ahead

When to Go

Sardinia is best known for its beaches, so most people go there in summer, but the weather is usually sunny and warm from mid-April through early October, and mild year-round. If possible, avoid August, when it may seem as though the entire population of all Italy's cities are in Sardinia.

TIME

L Sardinia is on Central European Time (GMT+1); summertime is in effect March to late October.

AVERAGE DAILY MAXIMUM TEMPERATURES

JAN	FEB	MAR	APR	MAY	JUN	JUL	AUG	SEP	OCT	NOV	DEC
10°C	11°C	13°C	19°C	22°C	25°C	31°C	31°C	26°C	22°C	16°C	12°C
50°F	52°F	55°F	66°F	72°F	77°F	88°F	88°F	79°F	77°F	61°F	54°F

Spring (March to May) March and April can be sunny or cloudy but warm. In May the clouds roll away and the pleasant temperatures remain.

Summer (June to August) June is idyllic, warm and sunny. In July and August it can be brutally hot, especially inland where the sea breezes don't keep the air cooled.

Autumn (September to November) September is warm and sunny. During October and November the temperatures start to drop and the rains begin.

Winter (December to February) January is the rainiest month, with December and February close behind. High in the mountains, snow is common in mid-winter.

WHAT'S ON

January *Feast of Sant'Antonio Abate*: celebrated across the island with bonfires. In Mamoiada costumed grotesque *mamathones* and *issohadores* parade.

February *Sa Sartiglia* (Sun and Tue before Lent): equestrian event in Oristano with medieval pageantry and costume.

April *Sa Die de Sa Sardigna* (28–29 Apr): Cágliari's costumed re-enactments of a 1794 rebellion with concerts and folkloric shows.

May *Festa di Sant'Efiso* (1–4 May): elaborate procession from Cágliari to Nora; massive pageant of costumes, horses and music.

Cavalcada Sarda (next to last Sun): costumes, horse events, folkloric music and dancing in Sássari.

July *L'Árdia di San Costantino* (6–8 Jul): at Sèdilo, 100 horsemen engage in a frenetic race to commemorate Constantine's victory in AD312.

August *Faradda di Li Candaleri*: Sássari procession, dating back to the 12th century, with huge dancing wooden columns parading amid pomp and music.

Festa del Redentore (last week): Núoro's religious pageantry and civic celebrations with parades, processions, costumes, music.

September *Festa di San Miquel Alghero* (28 Sep): fireworks and parades.

October *Sagra della Castagne Aritzo* (last Sun): Chestnut Fair.

November *Sagra dello Zafferano*: Villanovafranca celebrates Sardinia's 'red gold'—saffron.

December *Precipie*: nativity scenes, from miniature to life-sized, spring up indoors and out all over the island.

Sardinia Online
www.sardegnaturismo.it

Sardinia's official website is especially good for its itineraries, outlining routes for various interests, from gastronomic (such as saffron) to specific archaeological and artistic subjects. The events calendar can be searched by date to see what's on all over the island on any day.

http://visit-cagliari.it
Cágliari's official tourism website in English includes information on each of the historic quarters, with maps and details on places of interest, such as the Roman amphitheatre, listed under 'monuments'.

www.provinciadelsole.it
The official website for the province of Cágliari, which includes a large area of southern Sardinia, includes detailed information on individual towns. Some of the most complete information on San Sperate, for example, is found here. Most entries are translated into English, although not all.

www.holidays-in-sardinia.com
Not only is this site the best one-stop shop for lodging in B&Bs, *agriturismo* accommodation, inns and resorts, but it also has excellent information on travel, from ferries or flights to sailing excursions. It's a reliable resource for room reservations, car rental and activities, as well as information on towns all over the island. It is especially strong on agrotourism and characterful small hotels and inns, with more detailed descriptions and photographs than most places' own websites. Specials and last-minute deals.

www.stonepages.com/sardinia
Anyone fascinated (and who wouldn't be?) by Sardinia's prehistoric sites should browse this site for maps, pictures, descriptions and details about Nuraghe towers and villages, giants' tombs, necropoli, sacred wells and other sites.

PRIME TRAVEL SITE
www.fodors.com
A complete travel-planning site. You can research prices and weather; book air tickets, cars and rooms; ask questions (and get answers) from fellow travellers; and find links to other sites.

INTERNET ACCESS
Lamari Internet Cafe
✉ Via Napoli 43, at Via Sicilia, Cágliari ☎ 070 668 407 🕐 Mon–Sat 9–1, 4–8.30 💶 €5.00 per hour

Internet Point Centro Servizi Turistici
✉ Via Nazionale 18, Cannigione (Costa Smeralda) ☎ 368 351 9386 🕐 May–Sep Mon–Sat 9–1; Oct–Apr Mon–Fri 9–12.30, 3–6 💶 10 min €1.50, 1 hour €6

Net Gate di Valeria Fadda
✉ Piazza Università 4, Sássari ☎ 079 237 894 🕐 Mon–Sat 9–1, 5–8.30 💶 €5 per hour

Inter Smeraldo Internet Point
✉ Via Porto Romano 8b, Ólbia ☎ 078 925 366 🕐 Daily all year

Web Copy
✉ Piazza IV Novembre, Bosa 🕐 Mon–Sat 9–1, 5–8.30 💶 €5 per hour

Getting There

ENTRY REQUIREMENTS

Visitors from EU countries, the USA and Canada need only a passport to enter Italy, unless they plan to stay longer than 90 days, in which case a residence permit or special visa is required. For the latest information visit www.britishembassy.gov.uk or http://travel.state.gov. Be sure to carry your passport with you when driving a car.

INSURANCE

Although travellers from EU countries can receive emergency medical care at public facilities by presenting their European health card (EHIC), it is advisable for all visitors to carry health and travel insurance for the duration of their trip. The EHIC is not good for non-emergencies, at private clinics or for dental emergencies. Nor will it cover the cost of medical evacuation home.

AIRPORTS

Sardinia has three airports with regular commercial flights from the continent and elsewhere. All airports have all the usual facilities: tourist information, ATMs, car rental offices and cafés. For private transfers from any island airport, visit www.holidays-in-sardinia.com.

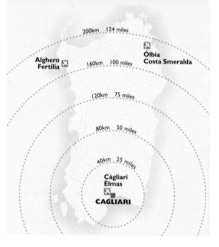

AEROPORTO CÁGLIARI ÉLMAS

Cágliari's Élmas Airport (☎ 079 211 211; www.aeroportodicagliari.com) is the main one for the southern part of Sardinia, served year-round by the national carriers Meridiana, Air One-Alitalia, British Airways, easyJet, Lufthansa, Ryanair and other airlines and seasonally by several others. ARST and CTM buses connect the main bus station at the port in Cágliari with Élmas airport daily every half-hour beginning at 6am; buy tickets before boarding from the small machine opposite the tourist information desk in the arrivals hall, or at the station in Cágliari. A taxi from central Cágliari to the airport is about €25 (☎ 070 400 101).

AEROPORTO ÓLBIA COSTA SMERALDA

Ólbia Costa Smeralda Airport (☎ 0789 563 400; www.geasar.it) is the main access hub for the Costa Smeralda, served in the summer

(May–Oct) by Meridiana, Air One, Austrian, CSA Czech, easyJet, Ryanair, Iberia, Air Berlin and a large number of others. Bus No. 2 (Mon–Sat) or No. 10 (daily) leaves Ólbia airport every half-hour between 7.30am and 7.30pm.

AEROPORTO ALGHERO FERTILIA

Alghero's Fertilia Airport (☎ 079 935 282; www.aeroportodialghero.it) is served by Air One flights from Palma, Ibiza, Tunis and Sicily, as well as from major cities in Italy, with Milan the most important connector. Ryanair also serves this airport from several continental cities and from London's Stansted. Regular ARST buses connect the airport to the city (journey time about 20 minutes).

ARRIVING BY BOAT

While smaller ferry lines with one or two routes each also connect Sardinia to the mainland, most visitors arrive by using the following two major ferry companies:

Tirrenia: ☎ 070 666 065; www.tirrenia.it
Genoa–Arbatax: 20 hours ⊙ Twice weekly, reduced winter
Genoa–Ólbia: 13.5 hours ⊙ Four weekly, reduced winter
Genoa–Porto Tórres: 9 hours ⊙ Twice daily Aug
Civitavecchia–Ólbia: 5–7.5 hours ⊙ Twice daily Jun to mid-Sep
Civitavecchia–Arbatax: 10.5 hours ⊙ Twice weekly
Civitavecchia–Cágliari: 13 hours ⊙ Daily
Napoli–Cágliari: 15.25 hours ⊙ Twice weekly
Trápani (Sicily)–Cágliari: 10 hours ⊙ Twice weekly Oct–Dec, once weekly Jan–Sep
Palermo (Sicily)–Cágliari: 11.5 hours ⊙ Once weekly
Moby: ☎ 199 303 040; www.moby.it
Genoa–Ólbia ⊙ Mid-Mar to Jan
Genoa–Porto Tórres ⊙ Late May–Sep
Livorno–Ólbia: 6 hours ⊙ Year-round
Piombino–Ólbia: 4.5 hours ⊙ Year-round
Piombino/Livorno–Ólbia ⊙ Apr–Oct
Civitavecchia–Ólbia: 5 hours ⊙ Mar–Sep

CAR RENTAL

Most major companies are represented at Cágliari and other airports, but it is important to reserve in advance, especially in the tourist season. At Cágliari airport, exit the arrivals hall to the right, following signs for *autonoleggi*, to a series of small kiosks across the access road.

Getting Around

ORGANIZED SIGHTSEEING

Apart from trekking excursions into the mountains, Sardinia has surprisingly few tours available, and public transport is not designed for tourists, especially to the prehistoric sites. By far the best way to visit without a car, or to get an informative tour of historic and artistic sites, is with a licensed professional guide. For tours of the Cágliari area or anywhere on the island, contact Paola Loi ☎ 338 266 1320.

BICYCLES

Apart from the Sínis Peninsula and a few other areas, much of the island rises to steep mountains, so roads provide a serious workout for cyclists. Do not expect drivers to make accommodation for cyclists, and beware that verges often have very sharp drop-offs at the edge of the tarmac surface. Bicycles can be brought on board ferries to Sardinia or rentals are available in resort areas and larger cities.

IN CÁGLIARI

Cágliari sits on a series of steep hills that rise from the wide port where ferries arrive from the mainland. Driving is difficult in its steep, narrow and winding streets, so it is best to leave a car in the large parking area (€) at the maritime station and walk or use the bus. The CTM (☎ 070 209 1200; www.ctmcagliari.it) bus station is just west of the port, on Piazza Matteotti, and tickets should be purchased in advance from machines there or at any newsstand. Insert the ticket in the meter for an imprint as you board. Day passes are also available at the station, but unless you plan to use the buses frequently it is better to use tickets.

Limited Traffic Zones Be aware that the Castello and many other downtown areas of Cágliari are within the ZTL–Zona a Trafico Limitato (Limited Traffic Zone). At the entrance to these there will be a large sign with a red circle and times shown beneath it. The crossed hammer symbol means that this applies to these hours only on working days (Mon–Sat), not to Sundays and holidays. Within those times it is strictly forbidden to drive within the zone. Your car will be photographed and traced to your address or the rental agency, which will charge the fine to your credit card. If you stay at a hotel within a ZTL, be sure that they call the police to get your car exempted.

Taxis It is not possible to flag down a taxi; they must be called in advance (☎ 0700 400 101, 070 6655) or found at one of the few ranks, located beside the town hall or at the other end of Largo Carlo Felice, near the statue. A taxi from the airport to the port is about €25. As anywhere, insist that the meter is running at the beginning of the ride or agree on a rate ahead of time for longer trips.

BUSES

ARST buses (☎ 800 655 042; http://arst.sardegna.it) connect the cities and many

smaller towns, but their schedules are rarely useful for sightseeing. Their user-friendly website allows you to click on any town and see bus schedules to any other. In the Ólbia area buses are operated by ASPO (☎ 0789 553 800; www.aspo.it). Bus services are almost non-existent on Sunday in many regions.

DRIVING

Driving is on the right, a challenge for those from left-driving countries. Be especially cautious when entering roundabouts and coming onto main roads from smaller ones. Mountain roads are steep and narrow, although they are usually in good repair. In some places roads narrow to a single lane and approaching cars must pull into a layby to pass. Italian law requires the use of headlamps at all times of day and seatbelts. When entering Autostada Carlo Felice (SS131), the nearest towns may not be marked on signs. North will always be marked 'Sássari' and south 'Cágliari', the cities at each end of the motorway.

PARKING

As elsewhere in Italy, free parking spaces are marked by white lines, but these may have time limits posted (set the disc found on the windscreen for the time you arrive). Spaces marked in yellow are reserved for locals and those in blue require payment. Look for a nearby ticket machine, but be sure to check the hours, as payment is only required at certain times. Saturday morning is considered a working day for parking fees.

TRAINS

Ferrovie della Sardegna (☎ 070 570 355; www.ferroviesardegna.it) trains connect some cities, including Cágliari, Ólbia, Témpio Pausánia, Sássari and Alghero, and are useful in getting between those cities, but not for seeing the island's major sights. The train station in Cágliari is on Piazza Matteotti.

Essential Facts

EMERGENCY NUMBERS

● Caribinieri (National Police) 112
● Local police 113
● Fire 115
● Automobile breakdown 116
● Ambulance 118

MONEY

The euro (€) is the unit of currency used in Sardinia. Notes come in denominations of €5, €10, €20, €50, €100, €200 and €500, and coins in 1, 2, 5, 10, 20, 50 cents, and €1 and €2. ATM cash dispensers are common; many small restaurants and shops don't take credit cards; travellers' cheques usually need to be cashed at banks.

€5

€10

€50

€100

ELECTRICITY

● The current throughout the island is 220 volts AC, and sockets take the circular two-pin continental-style plug.

EMBASSIES AND CONSULATES

● British Embassy ✉ Via XX Settembre, Rome ☎ 06 4220 0001; http://ukinitaly.fco.gov.uk 🕐 By appointment only
● Canadian Embassy ✉ Via Zara 30, Rome ☎ 06 85444 2911; emergency 06 854 441 🕐 Emergency services only Mon–Fri 9–4
● United States Embassy ✉ Corso Via Veneto and Via Boncompagni, Rome ☎ 06 4674 2190; http://italy.usembassy.gov 🕐 Mon–Fri 8.30–12.30
● French Consulate ✉ Piazza Deffenu 9, Cágliari ☎ 070 664 272, 070 65769
● German Consulate ✉ Via R. Garcia 9, Cágliari ☎ 070 307 229

MEDICAL TREATMENT

● Oristano: Presidio Ospedaliero San Martino ✉ Via Fondazione Rockefeller ☎ 078 33171
● Cágliari: Ospedale S. Giovanni di Dio ✉ Via Ospedale ☎ 070 6091
● Cágliari: (Ambulance) Polizia Soccorso Pubblico XIII Rep. Mobile Sardegna Dirigente ✉ Viale Buon Cammino 11, Cágliari ☎ 070 651 152
● Ólbia: Ospedale Civico San Giovanni di Dio ✉ Via Gian Lorenzo Bernini and Via Borromeo, Ólbia ☎ 0789 552 200

MEDICINES

Bring a sufficient supply of any required medicines, in carry-on baggage if you are flying. Bring a copy of the generic prescription with you, since brand names may vary. Pharmacies are plentiful, and if closed will have the address of the nearest open one posted outside.

NATIONAL HOLIDAYS

● 1 Jan: New Year's Day
● 6 Jan: Epiphany

- Mar/Apr: Easter Monday
- 25 Apr: Liberation Day
- 1 May: Labour Day
- 2 Jun: Republic Day
- 15 Aug: Feast of the Assumption (*Ferragosto*)
- 1 Nov: All Saints (*Ognissanti*)
- 8 Dec: Feast of the Immaculate Conception (*Immacolata Concezione*)
- 25 Dec: Christmas Day

SENSIBLE PRECAUTIONS

While Sardinia is considered a safe place for travellers, the same precautions apply here as do anywhere. Conceal luggage and personal belongings in the boot of the car, don't leave valuables lying about in hotel rooms, don't flaunt large amounts of cash, stay in well-lit areas of cities at night and remember that if a deal sounds too good to be true, it probably is.

TOURIST OFFICES

- Sardinian Tourist Board/Cágliari Tourist Board ✉ Piazza Alcide de Gasperi 1, 2nd floor, Cágliari ☎ 070 677 8428; www.comune.cagliari.it
- Alghero: Ufficio Informazione Turistico ✉ Piazza Porta Terra 9 ☎ 0799 79054; www.comune.alghero.ss.it
- Costa Smeralda: Tourist Office Cannigione ✉ Via Orecchioi, Cannigione ☎ www.arzachena-costasmeralda.it 🕐 Jun–Oct
- Maddelena: Tourist Office La Maddelena ✉ Via XX Settembre, La Maddelena ☎ 0789 736 3221; www.lamaddalena.it
- Oristano: Pro Loco Associazione Turistica Oristanese ✉ Via Ciutadella de Menorca 8 ☎ 0783 70621; www.comune.oristano.it
- Arzachena: Turismo Arzachena ✉ Piazza Risorgimento ☎ 0789 844 055; www.arzachena-costasmeralda.it
- Sássari: Ente Provinciale del Turismo ✉ Via Sebastiano Satta 13 ☎ 079 200 8072; www.comune.sassari.it
- Ólbia: Consorzio Turistico Ólbia Gallura ✉ Via Regina Elena 52 ☎ 0789 26673, 0789 52104; www.olbiaturismo.it

TELEPHONES

Most public phones only work with phone cards, which are sold at bars, tobacconists, newsagents and post offices. Tear off the top corner before inserting into the phone for the first time. International calls require an international phone card, which is not inserted in the phone. Call the local number on the card and follow the prompts. Much cheaper for international and long-distance calls is the Tiscalicard, which is not inserted into the phone, but used with a scratch-off PIN number. To call a number in Sardinia from a mobile that has a non-Italian number, dial 0039 before the number.

OPENING TIMES

- Shops: Usual shop hours are 9–1 and 4.30 or 5 until 8 or 8.30. Shops are normally open Saturday morning and closed on Sunday.
- Banks: Hours are irregular, but usually Monday to Friday, 8.30–1, 2.30–4

POST OFFICES

All cities and most towns have post offices; the main office in Cágliari is at Piazza Carmine. They are normally open Mon–Fri 8.30–1 in towns and 8.30–6.30 in cities, plus Saturday mornings.

Language

The Sardinian language is a melting pot of many influences. Around Alghero you will hear Catalan for example, which is no surprise, since hundreds of years of Spanish rule have left their mark. However, if there is one language from which *sardo* takes its roots, it is Latin; it is much closer to this mother tongue than mainland Italian is. Examples include *domus* (house), which is used in the Sard language in place of the Italian *casa*.

USEFUL WORDS AND PHRASES

yes/no	*si/non*
please	*per favore/piacere*
thank you	*grazie*
you're welcome	*prego/di niente*
good morning	*buon giorno*
good afternoon/ evening	*buona sera*
good night	*buona notte*
hello/goodbye	*ciao (informal)*
I don't understand	*non capisco*
do you speak English?	*parla inglese?*
I'm sorry	*mi dispiace*
how are you?	*come sta?*
I'm fine, thank you	*bene, grazie*
excuse me	*scusi*
I would like	*vorrei*
open/closed	*aperto/chiuso*
today/tomorrow	*oggi/domani*
left/right	*sinistra/destra*

MONEY

bank	*banco*
exchange office	*cambio*
money	*denaro*
post office	*posta*
traveller's cheque	*assegno di viaggio*
do you accept credit cards?	*accettate carte di credito?*
how much?	*quanto costa?*
it's too expensive	*è troppo caro*
it's cheap	*non è caro*

ACCOMMODATION

hotel	*albergo*
room	*camera*
one/two nights	*una notte/due notti*
for one/two people	*per una persona/*
	per due persone
with/without	*con/senza*
bath/shower	*bagno/doccia*
with air-conditioning	*con ania condizionata*
with a balcony	*con una terrazza*
does that include	*è inclua la prima*
breakfast?	*colazione?*
camp site	*un camping*
youth hostel	*ostello per la gioventù*

EATING OUT

I'd like to book a table	*Vorrei prenotore un tavolo*
do you have a table for two?	*avete un tavola per due?*
dish of the day	*menu a prezzo fisso*
wine list	*lista dei vini*
red/white wine	*vino rosso/bianco*
water	*acqua*
coffee	*caffè*
milk	*latte*
bread	*pane*
meat	*carne*
fish	*pesce*
shellfish	*crostacei*
vegetables	*contorni*

TRANSPORT

aeroplane/airport	*aero/aeroporto*
bus	*autobus*
train	*treno*
car/car hire	*macchina/autonoleggi*
taxi	*taxi*
ferry	*traghetto*
bus station	*autostazione*
railway station	*stazione ferroviania*
ferry terminal	*stazione marittima*
ticket	*biglietto*
one way/return	*solo andata/andata e ritorno*

NEED TO KNOW LANGUAGE

Timeline

PREHISTORIC TIMES

Archaeological evidence shows that human occupation of Sardinia began about 500,000BC and trade with Corsica and France for local obsidian tools existed as early as 6,000BC. The use of metals arrived with the Copper Age about 3000BC, and by 2500BC bronze was worked and chambered tombs (giants' tombs) built.

1700–900BC Nuraghic megalithic structures appear and attain their classic conical shape. Multi-towered Nuraghi built, well temples constructed.

900–200BC Phoenicians establish trading settlements in Sardinia, introducing urbanism and a written language. Carthage conquers the island.

238BC Rome defeats Carthage; the island becomes the first Roman province.

AD477–711 Vandals, Romans, Byzantines and Saracens invade. Christianity takes root; the first martyrs recognized.

1000–1250 Byzantine Judex system establishes the four Giudicati kingdoms of Cágliari, Arborea, Tórres and Gallura. Pisa and Genoa become dominant powers. Romanesque architecture introduced.

1297 The Spanish from Aragon and Catalonia create Kingdom of Sardegna and Corsica, which lasts 300 years.

1708 Spain loses the island to English and Austrians.

1720 The Duke of Piedmont is crowned the first king of all Sardinia and the island is ruled by a viceroy.

1820–1835 A land reform act, the

From left: Remains of a cone tower, Nuraghe Losa; Santissima Trinità de Saccargia, south of Sássari; archaeological site at Thárros; Torre Longosardo tower, Santa Teresa di Gallura; Sardinian flag, Cágliari; statue of Vittorio Emanuele, Sássari

Enclosures Act, making all common lands into private lands, creates unrest and results in use of stone from monolithic structures for walls to enclose land. A second law abolishes feudalism.

1847 At the urging of Sardinia the island is united politically with Piedmont.

1861 The King of Piedmont and Sardinia, Vittorio Emanuele II, becomes the king of Italy, which brings to an end the Kingdom of Piedmont and Sardinia.

1915 Italy enters World War I as an Ally. Sássari Brigade honoured for bravery in the trenches and members return home as progressive politicians opposed to Mussolini's Fascists.

1943 With Italy a member of the Axis in World War II, Allied bombing heavily damages Cágliari.

1948 Sardinia becomes an autonomous region.

1962 The Aga Khan develops the Costa Smeralda resort area.

1985 Sardinian Francesco Cossiga becomes president of Italian Republic.

2010 Centre-left politicians propose that the island become a nuclear-free zone.

NAPOLEONIC AGE

Young Napoleon attempted to seize La Maddalena Island in 1792, but failed. When the army of the French Republic invaded Piedmont in 1795, King Charles III of Piedmont and Sardegna sought refuge in Sardinia. In 1804–05 the island hosted the fleet of Admiral Horatio Nelson before its historic battle off Trafalgar in October 1805.

INTO THE HILLS

Repeated invasions and pirates drove inhabitants into Sardinia's rough interior. The island's reputation for banditry arose from their relative independence, need for self-reliance and reaction to the Enclosures Act of 1823, which abolished communal land rights.

Index

TWINPACK
Sardinia

WRITTEN BY Barbara Radcliffe Rogers and Stillman Rogers
COVER DESIGN Catherine Murray
DESIGN WORK Lesley Mitchell
INDEXER Marie Lorimer
IMAGE RETOUCHING AND REPRO Jackie Street
PROJECT EDITOR Apostrophe S Limited
SERIES EDITOR Marie-Claire Jefferies

Colour separation by AA Digital Department
Printed and bound by Leo Paper Products, China

A CIP catalogue record for this book is available from the British Library.

ISBN 978-0-7495-6808-5

Published by AA Publishing, a trading name of AA Media Limited, whose registered office is Fanum House, Basing View, Basingstoke, Hampshire RG21 4EA. Registered number 06112600.

Front cover image: AA/N Setchfield
Back cover images: (i) AA/N Setchfield; (ii) AA/C Sawyer; (iii) AA/N Setchfield; (iv) AA/N Setchfield

A04027
Maps in this title produced from mapping © Freytag-Berndt u. Artaria KG, 1231 Vienna-Austria

The Automobile Association would like to thank the following photographers, companies and picture libraries for their assistance in the preparation of this book.

Abbreviations for the pictures credits are as follows – (t) top; (b) bottom; (c) centre; (l) left; (r) right; (AA) AA World Travel Library.

1 AA/N Setchfield; 2-18 top panel AA/C Sawyer; 4 AA/N Setchfield; 5 AA/C Sawyer; 6tl AA/N Setchfield; 6tcl AA/N Setchfield; 6tcr AA/N Setchfield; 6tr AA/N Setchfield; 6bl AA/N Setchfield; 6bc AA/N Setchfield; 6br AA/N Setchfield; 7tl AA/N Setchfield; 7tcl AA/N Setchfield; 7tcr AA/N Setchfield; 7tr AA/N Setchfield; 7bl AA/N Setchfield; 7bc AA/N Setchfield; 7br AA/N Setchfield; 10t AA/N Setchfield; 10ct AA/N Setchfield; 10cb AA/N Setchfield; 10/11 AA/N Setchfield; 11t AA/N Setchfield; 11c AA/N Setchfield; 12t AA/N Setchfield; 12ct AA/N Setchfield; 12cb AA/N Setchfield; 12b AA/N Setchfield; 13t AA/J Tims; 13ct Brand X Pics; 13cb AA/M Bonnet; 13b AA/C Sawyer; 14t AA/N Setchfield; 14ct AA/N Setchfield; 14cb AA/N Setchfield; 14b AA/N Setchfield; 15 AA/N Setchfield; 16t AA/N Setchfield; 16c AA/N Setchfield; 16b AA/N Setchfield; 17t AA/N Setchfield; 17c AA/N Setchfield; 17b AA/N Setchfield; 18t AA/C Sawyer; 18c AA/N Setchfield; 18b AA/N Setchfield; 19i AA/N Setchfield; 19ii AA/N Setchfield; 19iii AA/N Setchfield; 19iv AA/N Setchfield; 19v AA/N Setchfield; 20/21 AA/N Setchfield; 24r AA/N Setchfield; 24/25 AA/N Setchfield; 25t AA/N Setchfield; 25b AA/N Setchfield; 26l AA/N Setchfield; 26r AA/N Setchfield; 27l AA/N Setchfield; 27c AA/N Setchfield; 27r AA/N Setchfield; 28l AA/N Setchfield; 28r AA/N Setchfield; 29l AA/N Setchfield; 29cl AA/N Setchfield; 29cr AA/N Setchfield; 29r AA/N Setchfield; 30l AA/N Setchfield; 30/31 AA/N Setchfield; 31t AA/N Setchfield; 31b AA/N Setchfield; 32-35 top panel AA/N Setchfield; 32 CuboImages srl/Alamy; 33 Ken Gillham/ Robert Harding; 34l MARKA/Alamy; 34r AA/N Setchfield; 35l AA/N Setchfield; 35r AA/N Setchfield; 36 AA/N Setchfield; 37 AA/N Setchfield; 38, 60t, 75t, 89t, 104 AA/N Setchfield; 39, 60c, 61t, 75c, 89c, 105 AA/N Setchfield; 40, 61c, 62, 76, 90, 106 AA/C Sawyer; 41 AA/C Sawyer; 44l AA/N Setchfield; 44/45t AA/N Setchfield; 44/45b AA/N Setchfield; 45b AA/N Setchfield; 46t AA/N Setchfield; 46b AA/N Setchfield; 47t AA/N Setchfield; 47b AA/N Setchfield; 48 AA/C Sawyer; 49 AA/C Sawyer; 50l AA/N Setchfield; 50c AA/N Setchfield; 50r AA/N Setchfield; 51l CuboImages srl/Alamy; 51r AA/N Setchfield; 52l AA/N Setchfield; 52r AA/N Setchfield; 53l CuboImages srl/Alamy; 53r Lonely Planet Images/Alamy; 54-57 top panel AA/N Setchfield; 54 AA/N Setchfield; 55 AA/N Setchfield; 56r AA/N Setchfield; 56l AA/N Setchfield; 57 AA/N Setchfield; 58 Lonely Planet Images/ Alamy; 59 john norman/Alamy; 63 AA/N Setchfield; 66l AA/N Setchfield; 66tr AA/N Setchfield; 66br AA/N Setchfield; 67t AA/N Setchfield; 67b AA/N Setchfield; 68 AA/N Setchfield; 68/69 AA/N Setchfield; 69t AA/N Setchfield; 69c AA/N Setchfield; 70l CuboImages srl/Alamy; 70r LOOK Die Bildagentur der Fotografen GmbH/ Alamy; 71l AA/N Setchfield; 71r AA/N Setchfield; 72-73 top panel AA/N Setchfield; 72 AA/N Setchfield; 73l AA/N Setchfield; 73r AA/N Setchfield; 74 AA/N Setchfield; 77 flashover/Alamy; 80 AA/C Sawyer; 81 AA/N Setchfield; 82l AA/N Setchfield; 82r AA/N Setchfield; 83l Lonely Planet Images/Alamy; 83r Imagebroker/Alamy; 84 AA/N Setchfield; 85-87 top panel AA/N Setchfield; 85 Bart Nedobre/Alamy; 86l AA/N Setchfield; 86r AA/N Setchfield; 87 AA/N Setchfield; 88 AA/N Setchfield; 91 AA/N Setchfield; 94l AA/N Setchfield; 94r AA/N Setchfield; 94/95 AA/N Setchfield; 95l AA/N Setchfield; 95r AA/N Setchfield; 96l Courtesy of the Cooperativa Archeotur; 96r AA/N Setchfield; 97l AA/N Setchfield; 97c AA/N Setchfield; 97r AA/N Setchfield; 98l AA/N Setchfield; 98c AA/N Setchfield; 98r AA/N Setchfield; 99l AA/N Setchfield; 99r AA/N Setchfield; 100-101 top panel AA/N Setchfield; 100 LOOK Die Bildagentur der Fotografen GmbH/Alamy; 101l AA/N Setchfield; 101r AA/N Setchfield; 102 AA/N Setchfield; 103 AA/N Setchfield; 107 AA/N Setchfield; 108-112 top panel AA/C Sawyer; 108i AA/N Setchfield; 108ii AA/A Mockford & N Bonetti; 108iii AA/N Setchfield; 108iv AA/N Setchfield; 108v AA/N Setchfield; 113 AA/N Setchfield; 114-125 top panel AA/N Setchfield; 120 European Central Bank; 122c AA/N Setchfield; 122b AA/N Setchfield; 124l AA/N Setchfield; 124c AA/N Setchfield; 124r AA/N Setchfield; 125l AA/N Setchfield; 125c AA/N Setchfield; 125r AA/N Setchfield.

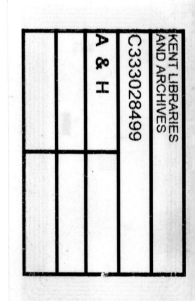